UNDERSEA VEHICLES AND HABITATS

BY THE AUTHOR

Burning Lands and Snow-Capped Mountains:
The Story of the Tropics

Experimental Planes:
Subsonic and Supersonic

Flashing Harpoons:
The Story of Whales and Whaling

Ice Island:
The Story of Antarctica

Stories of the States

Undersea Vehicles and Habitats:
The Peaceful Uses of the Ocean

Undersea vehicles and habitats

THE PEACEFUL USES OF THE OCEAN

By Frank Ross, Jr.

Illustrated with Photographs

THOMAS Y. CROWELL COMPANY
NEW YORK

For Martha and Tibor with warm affection.

Published simultaneously in Canada by
Fitzhenry & Whiteside, Limited, Toronto.
Designed by Wladislaw Finne
Manufactured in
the United States of America
L.C. Card 76-106577

1 2 3 4 5 6 7 8 9 10

Introduction

This is a book about a new class of submarines (submersibles), diving chambers, and manned ocean-floor stations. These engineering developments, tools really, are being used by man in a rapidly growing effort to learn more about the seas. Oceanographic activities were once limited largely to the surface of the oceans, but now these new devices are making it possible as never before to penetrate and explore the deep inner world of the seas. With their help, man is returning to an environment from which he emerged millions of years ago.

The underwater engineering developments described here represent only the beginning in what promises to be a large and varied family of such devices in the future. In this respect they are much like the newly created satellites and spacecraft with which the world of outer space is being explored. The submersibles, diving chambers, and manned underwater stations now in existence anticipate a time when the ocean depths will be worked and lived in with almost the same freedom as the land surfaces are inhabited now.

It may be noticed that no attempt has been made to discuss in depth the naval submarine in the chapters that follow. This type of undersea vessel, long in operation, is a story by itself. The main concern here is with the unique deep-ocean vehicles and underwater equipment created for peaceful purposes. This is the exciting new world unfolding in oceanography today.

Contents

1. Diving History 1
2. Diving for Science 39
3. Work Submersibles 79
4. Ocean Habitats and Diving Chambers 107
5. Submersibles and Habitats of The Twenty-first Century 143

A Glossary of Some Oceanographic Terms 173

Suggested Further Reading 176

Index 178

Diving for coral in Sicily about 1600. (National Maritime Museum, Greenwich, England)

Chapter 1
Diving history

Human life began in the seas several million years ago. Over an infinitely long period, land-bound man slowly took form. Although no longer physically capable of moving about in the marine world as easily as he once could, man has never truly lost his primordial heritage of the seas. He has always turned to the seas for food, treasure, commerce, and making war against his fellow man.

Relics of ancient civilizations tell us that underwater diving was going on some 4,000 years before the birth of Christ. Much evidence of this is found in the Mediterranean region. But diving in ancient times was certainly not confined to this part of the world. It was practiced also by early man in the Americas and the Orient.

Diving in ancient times required skill and endurance. Breathing deeply to fill his lungs with an extra supply of air, the underwater swimmer plunged naked into the sea, often holding a heavy rock to help him get to the bottom faster. A rope fastened around the waist was his only connection with the surface. When his lungs were nearly emptied of air the diver would either yank the rope once or twice to signal his colleagues to pull him out of the water or he would make his own ascent up the rope, hand over hand.

Sponges, oysters (prized mostly for pearls), rare coral, and shells to make dye for coloring cloth were some of the objects sought by the ancient undersea divers. They also salvaged treasure from sunken ships. How deep could they go and how long could they remain underwater? Judging from the depths at which these objects are usually found, it has been estimated that ancient free divers could plunge as deep as 100 feet into the sea and remain submerged for as long as two or three minutes.

Despite the existence and use of a great deal of sophisticated underwater equipment today, free diving, as the ancients did it, is still widely practiced. This is particularly true in Japan and Korea, where colonies of women, about 30,000 of them, are employed to gather edible shellfish and seaweeds from the bottom of the sea. At one time men also engaged in this activity, but they were entirely replaced by women because female swimmers could endure the cold water better and stay submerged longer. Carrying on an industry that goes back to about the fourth century A.D., the Japanese and Korean female divers, called *ama,* work at an average depth of 15 to 20 feet for half a minute at a time. There are instances when they plunge to 80 feet for choice sea morsels. Except for the use of lead weights tied about their waists or held in their hands to hasten the descent and modern glass face masks, these divers are little different from their ancient counterparts.

Some inventive diver of the ancient world brought into existence one of the first pieces of equipment to aid the underwater swimmer. This was a hollow reed, one end of which a swimmer held in his mouth while the other end protruded above the surface of the water. This enabled the swimmer to breathe as he moved along beneath the sea.

A modern version of this device is the snorkel. This was originally an air-intake and exhaust tube extending upward from the hull of a submarine. German U-boats in World War II were equipped with snorkels that permitted them to remain just below the surface of the water far longer than submarines that did not have them. Later, a small air-breathing snorkel was developed, and it became popular with those who swim underwater for sport.

In one of many Greek legends about the sea, and diving in particular, the reed snorkel played a key role. Herodotus, a Greek historian, tells this story of Scyllis and his daughter Cyane. Both were from a family of celebrated divers. Scyllis and Cyane were also famous for their ability to swim underwater for long distances.

Xerxes, a powerful ruler of Persia, hired the father-and-daughter diving team to recover some valuable treasure that had gone to the bottom aboard Persian ships sunk in a battle with Greek naval vessels. Scyllis and Cyane accomplished what they had been asked to do, then waited to be rewarded for their efforts as Xerxes had promised. Instead, the Persian ruler not only failed to pay the divers but held them as prisoners aboard his ship. This angered the divers and, choosing an opportune moment during a storm, they dived overboard, used their knives to slash the anchor ropes of several of the Persian galleys, and then swam toward Greece.

The storm hurled some of the anchorless Persian ships against a rocky shore, while others were damaged and wrecked as they crashed into one another. The Persians became furious and pursued Scyllis and Cyane. But staying beneath the water, using hollow reeds for breathing, the divers swam safely to their homeland.

Diving for treasure aboard sunken ships had grown to be a widespread activity in the eastern Mediterranean world by 200 B.C. In Greece laws were passed that entitled divers to half the salvaged treasure when recovered from a depth of twenty-five feet, 30 percent of the treasure taken from twelve feet of water, and 10 percent when valuable objects were brought to the surface from a depth of less than three feet.

The snorkel was not the only aid to undersea diving known to the ancient world. The idea of descending into the watery depths safely enclosed within a compartment was also familiar to some peoples. History—or, more accurately, legend—says that one of the first to make a descent into the sea within a diving chamber was Alexander the Great (356–323 B.C.), conqueror of much of the ancient Western world. By his orders a glass barrel big enough to hold a man was constructed. With the aid of chains, Alexander had the barrel lowered into the sea. Of the wonders seen there, the conqueror told of a fish so big it took three days to swim past his glass diving bell. Furthermore, it traveled with the speed of lightning. Undoubtedly, this was the first of all the extraordinary fish stories that have followed since.

Aristotle, in his book *Problems,* tells a much more factual anecdote concerning Alexander and diving. In the era of this conqueror divers were

Alexander the Great underwater in a glass barrel. (National Maritime Museum, Greenwich, England)

often a small but elite group in the armies. They would swim underwater to unsuspecting enemy ships, and bore holes in their hulls or cut their anchor ropes. Divers were also used to build and destroy log barricades at the entrances to harbors. At the siege of Tyre in 332 B.C. Alexander the Great called upon his squad of divers to tear down an underwater barrier built by the defenders across the mouth of the harbor.

The "frogmen" units of World War II were a revival of this type of underwater activity. Equipped with rubber suits, artificial breathing apparatus, and explosives, the frogmen would swim beneath the sea on highly dangerous missions to blow up defense installations protecting enemy shore positions. Frogmen of the United States armed forces were particularly useful in the Pacific war, where their advance demolition work paved the way for troops invading Japanese-held islands.

Diving, as practiced in ancient times, remained little changed for centuries. Few if any new ideas were advanced for safely prolonging a diver's stay beneath the water. It was not until the early decades of the 1500's that diving began a new era of development. In this and succeeding centuries, many inventive minds in Europe and America produced countless new ideas to enable man to carry on activities beneath the sea. These schemes fell into two broad groups: One had to do with underwater chambers and vehicles; the other was involved with equipment that an individual diver might wear.

The great majority of these proposals were far-fetched and never got beyond the idea stage. Some that were carried out, while hardly practical from the standpoint of modern developments, at least had the value of inspiring others to improve them

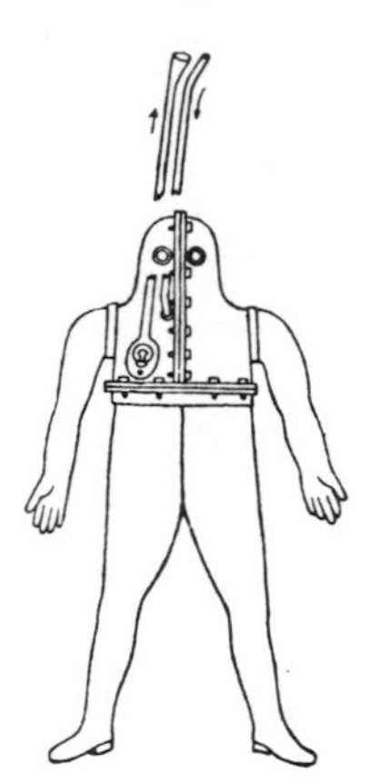

Some diving devices of the late eighteenth and early nineteenth centuries. (Siebe Gorman & Co., Ltd.)

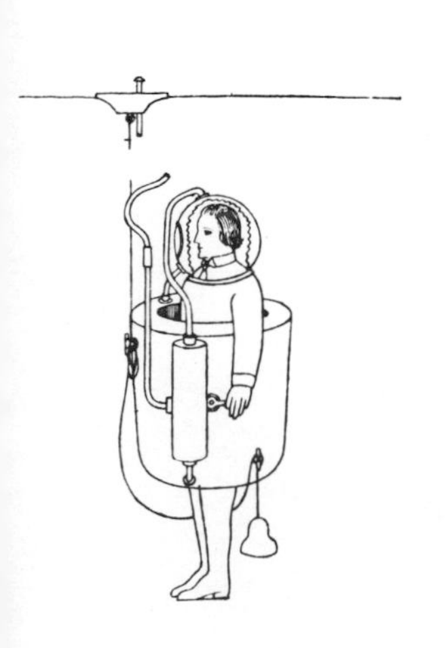

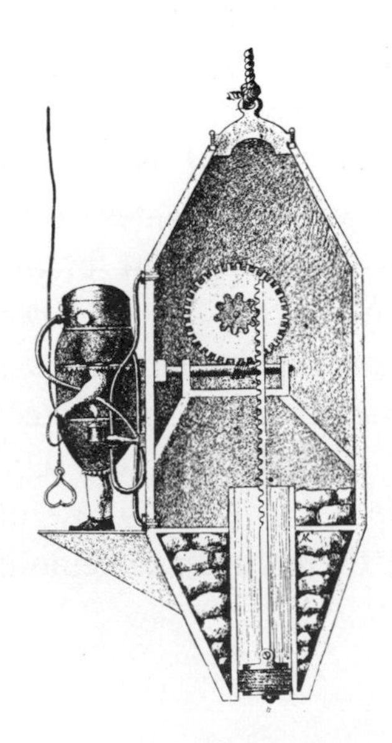

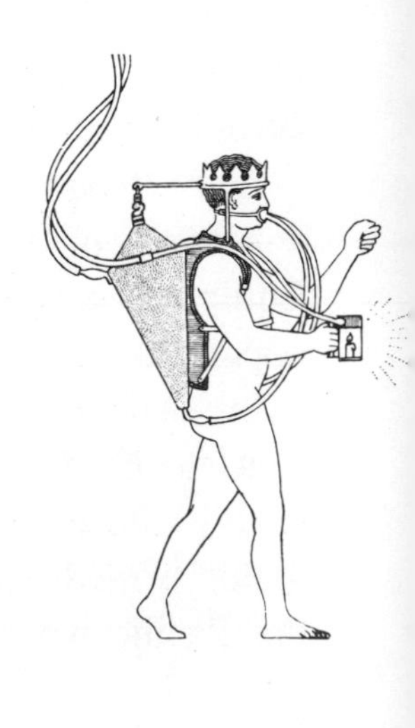

or to build better devices. Whatever their failings, many of the ideas and the designs actually constructed helped to lay the groundwork for the present advanced state of underwater technology.

The stationary diving bell was one of the first and more popular of the underwater devices to capture the interest of early inventors. In 1538 two Greek inventors demonstrated a diving bell in the Tagus River, Toledo, Spain. Emperor Charles V was among the audience of several thousand who lined the riverbanks for the event. All were certain that they were about to witness a double suicide.

The diving bell was made of bronze and large enough to hold the two inventors. They sat inside the lower, broad end of the bell on a wooden plank. Both held candles as the bell, open bottom end first, was lowered into the water. After about twenty minutes had passed, the bell was pulled up with the inventors alive and dry and the candles still burning.

Shouts of astonishment rose from the massed onlookers. Few, if any, realized that the feat was accomplished by the equalizing of air and water pressure within the bell. The bell was launched perfectly straight into the river so as not to lose its air supply, and the water entered the open end only to the point where the air pressure and the water pressure within the chamber would be the same. Depending on the depth to which the bell was lowered, the water could have risen inside a few inches or a foot or two.

The idea behind the successful demonstration of this Greek diving chamber can be duplicated by a simple home experiment. Take an empty glass, turn it upside down in a basin of water, and force it to the bottom. If the glass is held straight and no air permitted to escape, it will remain practically empty of water although completely submerged.

By the 1600's diving bells were beginning to appear in a number of countries throughout Europe. Both tinkerers and scientists were devoting their efforts to building improved types. Diving bells had long since passed from the novelty stage, as devices for stunt performers, to valuable tools for practical underwater work. Some of the tasks for which they were employed included salvaging treasure and cannon from sunken ships, working on the underwater sections of lighthouses and bridges, and repairing ships' hulls.

In 1616 a German, Franz Kessler, built a free diving chamber that required no ropes for lowering or raising it in the water. A diver using it carried heavy weights—cannonballs usually—for descending to the sea bottom. When his air supply was exhausted the diver discarded the weights, which made the chamber lighter and more buoyant, causing it to rise slowly to the surface.

Kessler's diving chamber was a wooden, bell-shaped structure with an outer covering of leather to help make it watertight. Glass portholes through which the diver could observe the underwater world circled the upper portion. Kessler's diving bell was an advance over those generally in use because it did not require a rope to lower it into the water or to pull it upward. However, a diver using it had to be extremely careful not to trip and fall while on the sea bottom. Were this to happen, the air within the bell would be replaced with water, drowning the diver in short order.

Another important milestone in the develop-

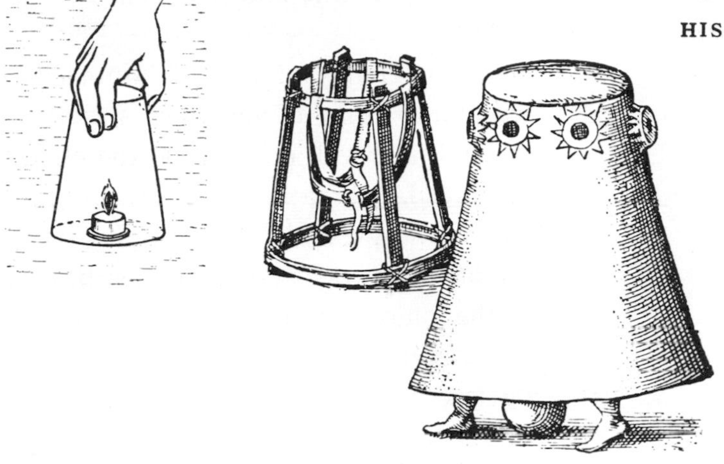

Franz Kessler's diving bell of 1616. As in all such underwater devices of that time, water was kept out by the air supply trapped inside. A drinking glass turned upside down in water illustrates the principle. A diver using the Kessler bell sat within the frame unit shown next to the bell. (Siebe Gorman & Co., Ltd.)

ment of diving bells came in 1689 as the result of work by Dr. Denis Papin, a French scientist. He thought up a scheme for supplying continuous fresh air to divers inside underwater chambers by pumping it from the surface through tubes. Unfortunately Dr. Papin's idea was ahead of its time, because there were no adequate pumps then in existence for creating the proper air supply.

His idea was put to use, however, by one of the more interesting of the early inventors of underwater chambers—Sir Edmund Halley, a doctor and famous astronomer (he discovered the comet that bears his name). Halley was also ahead of his time, by 300 years, in that he combined an interest in the world of outer space with an interest in the world of the sea, where much of the more exciting scientific and technical news is occurring today.

It was Halley's medical training, however, that led him to build an improved, practical diving bell in 1690. He well understood the effects of bad air produced by breathing within a confined chamber. Rebreathing exhaled carbon dioxide can bring on unconsciousness and even death. This was one of the major factors limiting a diver's stay beneath the water within the early diving bells. Halley devised a method for bringing fresh air to his underwater chamber and for venting off the bad air created by its occupants.

The open diving chamber designed and built by Halley was made of wood and sheathed on its outside with lead to make it watertight and to give it weight for easy descent. A ring-shaped platform carrying three 100-pound weights was suspended by ropes from the bottom of the bell. This acted as an anchor, steadying the chamber while it was on the sea bottom.

The diving bell measured 5 feet across the open bottom's diameter and 3 feet at the top. At the top of the bell Halley installed a glass porthole so that on its trip underwater, some light would penetrate the darkened chamber. Also at the top was a valve attached to a long leather hose. The hose reached to the surface and carried off the bad air within the chamber.

Halley's method for bringing fresh air to the occupants of his diving bell was simple. Lead-lined barrels of air from a ship on the surface were lowered into the water near the chamber. Each barrel had two holes, one at the top and one at the bottom. A leather hose attached to the top hole of the barrel extended through the open bottom of the diving bell. As seawater entered the barrel by way of its bottom hole, water pressure forced the fresh air out of the top hole, through the hose, and into the diving bell. The English scientist's scheme worked with considerable success. As long as barrels of fresh air were supplied, the divers using the chamber could stay safely submerged even for long periods.

To increase the usefulness of his diving chamber, Halley also devised a crude helmet of leather which a diver wore and to which a leather hose was fastened. This connected the diver to his air supply within the chamber. Slipping out of the bottom of the diving bell to the floor of the sea, the diver could walk around limited only by the length of his air hose.

Demonstrating complete faith in his invention, Halley, along with four companions, descended some 60 feet into the water inside the chamber and remained submerged for an hour and a half. Diving chambers rarely went deeper than that in his day. Subsequently Halley's underwater invention was widely used for salvage work.

There were a number of inventors who believed that the open-end diving bell was not the complete answer for safely taking divers to the bottom of the sea. These vehicles were limited as to the depth they could reach and were extremely dangerous. They had to enter the water in a perfectly straight position and remain that way on the bottom. If the chamber accidentally tipped, the air supply would escape and be replaced with water. Several inventors felt that a closed chamber was the only way to get to and from the sea bottom and remain there without danger.

One of the earliest ideas on record for an undersea closed chamber was suggested by William Bourne, an English naval officer, late in the sixteenth century. Bourne's vehicle was to be made of wood and covered with leather for watertightness. But his proposal never got beyond the idea stage.

John Day, also of England, built another version of a closed diving chamber in 1772. Unfortunately the inventor drowned in his undersea device during a test dive.

Ultimately, those who believed the closed chamber was superior to the open chamber won out. While many early ideas related to closed diving chambers were sound, inventors were handicapped by inadequate materials and equipment for building their underwater devices. Water pressure made it difficult to build a watertight wooden diving bell. Water forced its way through the smallest opening. This was not too great a problem with the pioneering diving bells because they were used in shallow water, where the water pressure is not great. However, when inventors tried to build underwater chambers of wood for depths of a hundred feet and beyond, disaster resulted. Further, these inventors lacked an efficient means of supplying their diving bells with fresh air. Overcoming these problems had to wait for another age when stronger materials, like steel, became available, along with practical artificial air-supply systems.

The same difficulties faced by those building closed diving chambers were encountered by inventors who dreamed of creating a workable submarine. Proposals for building moving underwater vehicles can be traced as far back as the sixteenth century.

Among the first to advance an idea for a submarine was William Bourne, the English naval officer mentioned earlier.

The undersea boat conceived by Bourne in 1578 was to be made of wood and covered with leather. Adjustable leather chambers were to be located on both sides of the hull. These could be compressed or extended like an accordion by hand-operated screws, forcing water out of the chambers or permitting it to enter. The water passed through a series of holes in the sides of the hull. When these chambers were filled the boat was heavier; when they were empty the boat was lighter. This was to aid the submarine in diving and rising to the surface again. These chambers were the crude forerunners of the ballast tanks used by modern submarines.

This action illustrated Archimedes' principle of buoyancy. A floating object displaces as much water in weight as the object itself weighs. Thus if a submarine is given added weight it displaces more water and sinks. This is called negative buoyancy. If a submarine is made lighter, by blowing seawater from its ballast tanks, it displaces less water and rises. It is now in a state of positive buoyancy.

If a submarine is to travel at a particular depth beneath the sea, its weight is carefully adjusted by the filling of the ballast tanks so that it will not rise or sink. Its weight balances the weight of the water displaced at the desired depth. The submarine is now said to be neutrally buoyant. The submarine "hovers" at a certain depth when its engines are stopped or slowed so that the vessel is not moving.

When submerged a submarine may use its main

ballast system or an auxiliary system for adjusting its fore-and-aft balance (tipping forward or backward) and neutral buoyancy. Submariners call this "trimming."

Bourne's submarine, although never built, was also to have a tube extending from within the hull to above the deck. This was to bring fresh air to the crew while the vessel was submerged. The British naval officer thus anticipated the modern snorkel by more than 350 years.

Cornelis Drebbel, a Dutch physician and scientist living in England, was much more successful with his submarine invention in 1620. Facts are scarce about Drebbel's underwater vehicle, but it is known that he built two models of it. The larger was made of wood reinforced with iron bands and covered with leather. This was coated with grease to make it watertight. Drebbel's vehicle was able to descend to a depth of several feet and was propelled while underwater by twelve oarsmen, six on either side of the vessel. The oars were fitted snugly through leather sleeves so that water could not enter the hull. The submarine fore and aft was pointed and had room for six passengers in addition to the crew.

Drebbel successfully sailed his submarine a number of times beneath the surface of the Thames River. King James I even appeared one day on the riverbank to observe this marvelous creation.

Drebbel thought of his invention as a deadly weapon of war that could wreck an enemy fleet in a single day, regardless of the weather or the roughness of the seas. The British Admiralty, to whom Drebbel tried to sell his submarine, would have no part of it, however.

Another early attempt to build a practical submarine was made by a Frenchman, De Son, in 1653. This inventor's underwater vessel was also intended strictly for fighting purposes. Built of wood and iron, the submarine was 72 feet long, 12 feet high, and 8 feet wide. Both fore and aft it was equipped with sharply pointed iron rods. These were intended to be used as rams for crashing into and destroying enemy boats.

De Son's submarine had a most unusual propulsion system. This was a large paddle wheel installed in the center of the craft, its blades reaching down into the water. It was connected to a clock mechanism, which, when wound up, revolved the wheel. This is believed to be the first occasion that a paddle wheel was adapted for propelling a boat of any kind.

Just as Drebbel did, the French inventor claimed that his submarine could easily destroy a whole fleet of ships. "No fire, nor Storme, or Bullets, can hinder her, unless it please God." Furthermore, with the aid of its paddle wheel's driving force, he thought the vessel could travel to the East Indies in six weeks. In that age of slow, lumbering caravels and galleons, reaching the other side of the earth in less than two months would have been nothing short of miraculous.

De Son's submarine of 1635. (National Maritime Museum, Greenwich, England)

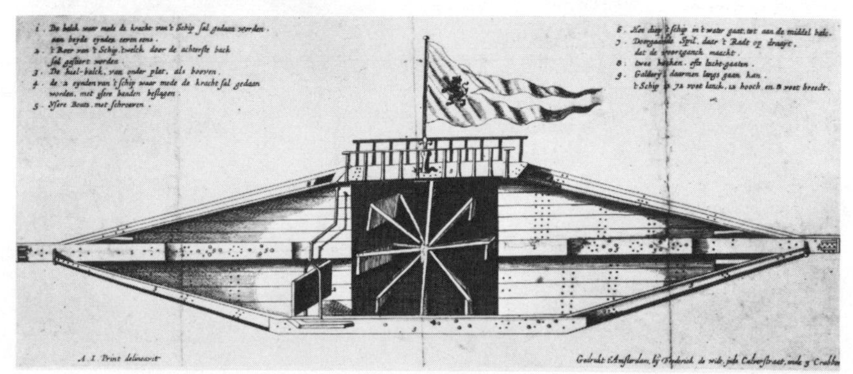

De Son first tried his paddle wheel and clock mechanism propulsion system on land, and it worked to his satisfaction. However, after he launched his submarine in the water and tried to start the paddle wheel, it was a different matter. The resistance of the water was far greater than the strength of the spring mechanism. It proved too weak to turn the wheel. Once again an idea had to be abandoned because it was too advanced for technical knowledge then in existence.

One of the most interesting chapters in the development of the submarine occurred in eighteenth-century America during the period of the Revolution. The chief actor was David Bushnell, a young Connecticut man. He conceived the idea for a submarine to surprise and harass British ships that were then sailing freely in and out of colonial ports. Bushnell brought his invention to General George Washington's attention. Grasping at every opportunity to defeat the British, the hard-pressed American general gave Bushnell the go-ahead to build the submarine.

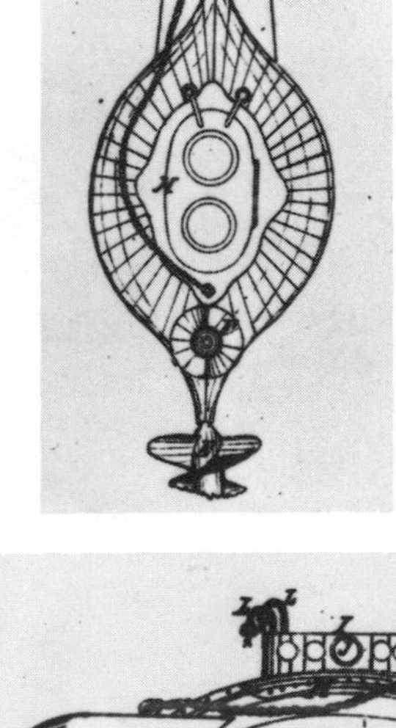

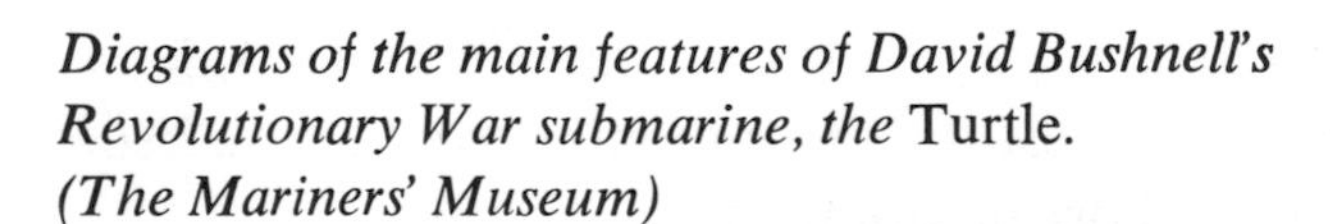

Diagrams of the main features of David Bushnell's Revolutionary War submarine, the Turtle.
(The Mariners' Museum)

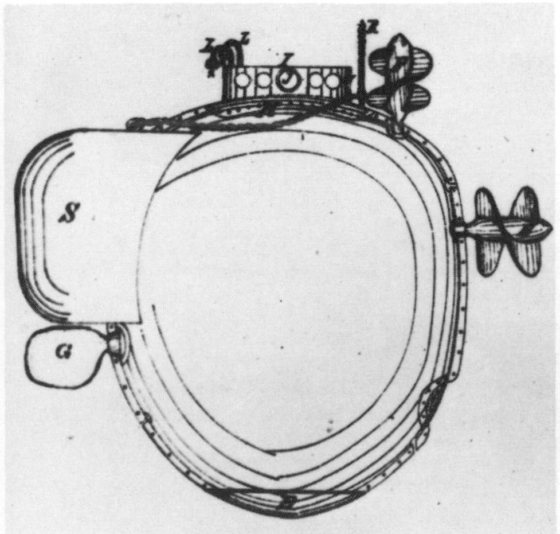

David Bushnell was a first-rate inventor and mechanic. His submarine, which he named the *Turtle,* had many features that were extremely advanced for the period. Built of wood sections firmly held together by iron straps, the *Turtle* had the shape of a giant chowder clam turned on edge. The wood sections were so tightly joined that there was hardly any leakage of water. The hull was 7½ feet long, large enough to accommodate a single crew member. At the top of the submarine was a short conning tower with a series of glass portholes around it. The one-man crew entered through the conning tower, and when he sat at his post inside, his eyes were at the level of the portholes.

The *Turtle*'s propulsion system included a screw propeller fixed to the front of the submarine. Inventors were just becoming familiar with this device for powering ships. Bushnell connected his propeller to a hand-crank within the submarine, which, when turned by the crew member, caused the undersea boat to move forward. A vertical propeller, also hand-cranked, was attached to the upper side of the *Turtle*. This was used to help the submarine rise to the surface after a descent. Bushnell was far ahead of his time with this device, which has been revived since and is a vital feature of certain present-day research and work submarines.

For plunging beneath the water and rising again, Bushnell installed ballast tanks aboard his submarine. A foot-operated valve allowed water to flow into the tanks when the *Turtle* was about to dive. A pump, also operated by foot action, forced the water out of the ballast tanks when the submarine was ready to rise. The ballast not only helped the *Turtle* to descend; it also held the craft upright.

A tank of air was installed inside for the single crew member. It was enough to permit him to remain beneath the water for about half an hour. Two short ventilator tubes extended up through the conning tower. One provided fresh air to the inside compartment when the *Turtle* was on the surface; the other was an escape vent for the bad air produced by the crewman's breathing.

When the *Turtle* was operating as a submarine, a portion of its conning tower, including the portholes, showed above the water. Thus the pilot could guide the craft simply by looking through one of the ports. Also to help his navigation, Bushnell installed a compass and pressure gauge. A small, hand-operated rudder extending rearward helped the pilot to steer his submarine. The *Turtle* could also travel completely submerged for short distances. Its top speed was about 3 knots, almost 4 miles per hour.

As a fighting submarine, the *Turtle* was equipped with a crude torpedo. Bushnell fashioned this out of two hollow logs jammed with 150 pounds of explosive powder. It was stowed on the rear of the submarine and held in place with rope. The torpedo was to be exploded by a clock mechanism after it was fastened to the underside of an enemy ship's hull. This was to be done with the help of a carpenter's drill, installed on the forward part of the submarine and operated from within. A screw fitting into the drilled hole would attach the underwater bomb to the ship. Because this operation would take some time, Bushnell instructed that the *Turtle* be used under cover of darkness.

Completing the midget submarine in the summer of 1776, the Connecticut inventor planned to send it into action against one of the British warships anchored in New York harbor. The night of September 6 was chosen for the dangerous mission, and the H.M.S. *Eagle,* flagship of the British fleet, was selected as the intended victim. Bushnell had wanted to pilot the *Turtle* himself, but illness forced him to select a colonial soldier who had volunteered for the risky assignment—Sergeant Ezra Lee.

After being carefully instructed in piloting the submarine and the manner in which the explosive was attached, Lee squeezed himself through the tiny opening of the *Turtle*'s conning tower. He was towed part way toward the *Eagle*. Then, with the help of a friendly tide and his own propelling action, Lee managed to maneuver the *Turtle* beneath the *Eagle* undetected. Working near the stern of the warship in darkness, the submariner began using the vertical drill.

To his dismay Lee discovered that the supposedly wooden hull was instead sheathed with copper. Try as he would, Lee could not puncture the metal with the drill. With dawn approaching, the American was forced to give up and head for the safety of land. Had he moved a few feet to the rear of the British vessel, near the stern post where wood was exposed, Sergeant Lee would have had better luck.

Moving away from the *Eagle* as fast as he could, Lee had trouble controlling his submarine in the strong tide. Instead of heading for Manhattan Island and safety, he was carried in the direction of Governors Island, where the British were strongly entrenched. Alert sentries spotted the strange vessel and soon a boat was sent out in pursuit. As the would-be captors drew dangerously close, Lee detached the explosive charge, set the firing mechanism, and hurled it in the path of the British.

The strategy worked. The explosive went off with a roar—frightening the pursuers, who gave up the chase. Lee, after much struggling with the controls, finally brought his submarine to the Manhattan shore.

Although the mission failed, Bushnell's *Turtle* was the first submarine to attempt the sinking of a surface ship.

At the turn of the eighteenth century another American, Robert Fulton, contributed further to submarine development. Fulton was talented at solving engineering problems as well as being an artist of some ability. The possibility of creating a submarine for military purposes had caught his interest years before he was to become famous as the builder of one of the earliest steamboats.

Fulton was in Paris at the time he worked on his submarine design. He tried to sell it to Napoleon for use as a surprise weapon against the British. After gaining the support of the French government Fulton constructed the submarine, which he named the *Nautilus*. Built with iron ribs and copper sheathing, it was 20 feet long and 7 feet wide when completed.

The submarine included features pioneered by David Bushnell. For example, a stern propeller was installed to operate the vessel when it was submerged. This was turned by a hand-crank within the submarine. Sails were used to power the craft when it was on the surface. Fulton borrowed another of Bushnell's ideas when he placed a tank of compressed air in the crew compartment. The stern end of the *Nautilus* was also equipped with horizontal rudders that helped the submarine to dive beneath the sea and rise again. This feature, Fulton's own, anticipated such devices on modern submarines by a hundred years.

The *Nautilus* was successfully tested in the Seine River in 1800 and later in the harbor of Le Havre, where an unsuccessful attempt was made to attack several British ships. Despite its promise as a naval weapon, the French government then lost interest in Fulton's submarine and refused to have anything further to do with it.

Another major development in the submarine's history came with the American Civil War. During that conflict Union naval forces were superior to the Confederates and were able to block most of the southern ports. In a desperate effort to break this stranglehold, the Confederates tried building submarines, which they called David boats.

Using iron plates that had once served as part of steam boilers aboard river paddle-wheel boats, several experimental submarines were built. All were disastrous failures, suffocating and drowning more than forty crewmen on test dives. Despite the mishaps, work on the underwater vessels continued, finally bringing the *H.L. Hunley* into existence.

Made of iron boiler plates like the previous models, the *Hunley* was cylindrical in shape and almost 40 feet long. Two hatchways, through which the crew entered the vessel, were located on the topside at the bow and stern. At the stern were a propeller and a vertical rudder. Near the bow on both sides of the hull were short horizontal fins, like the wings of an airplane. These helped to keep the submarine on an even keel when traveling submerged. Hampered as all early submarines were by the lack of an adequate engine for pro-

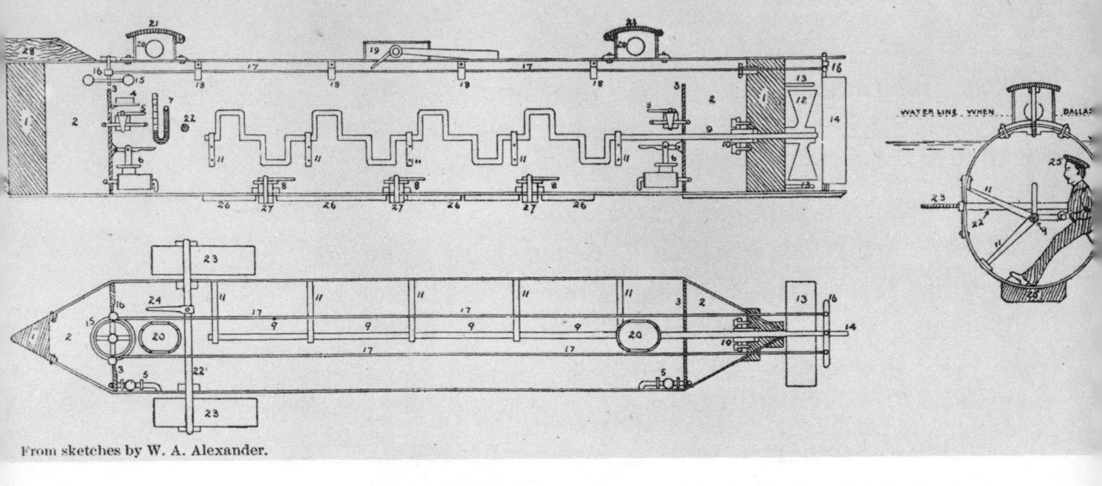

Interior arrangement of the Confederate submarine Hunley. *(The Mariners' Museum)*

pelling the craft underwater, the *Hunley* required human muscle power for turning its propeller. This was done by means of a long shaft extending from the propeller into the interior of the vessel. It was formed in a series of U-shaped bends. A nine-man crew took side-by-side positions to crank the shaft and were able to propel the sub at a top speed of 4 knots.

The *Hunley* was also given ballast tanks, which, when flooded with water, helped to submerge the craft. The depth to which it could plunge was controlled by iron weights. When the desired level was reached, a certain number of the weights were cast overboard to make the craft lighter and thus stabilize its position.

Like its predecessors, the *Hunley* was far from a success. Indeed, its performance was so poor that the volunteer crew who took it on test dives never felt sure of returning to the surface alive. Despite its shortcomings, Confederate naval authorities decided to use it in an attack on Union ships. Preparations were made to send it against the *Housatonic,* a Union warship of 1,200 tons that was helping to blockade Charleston harbor.

A 10-foot-long spar torpedo was attached to the *Hunley*'s bow. This was a hollow beam packed with ninety pounds of blasting powder. The torpedo was to be fixed to the hull of the Union ship and then exploded by a time fuse. The fuse would be set in such a way that the crew would have time to move the *Hunley* away before the charge went off.

The *Hunley* sailed toward its intended victim as night settled over Charleston harbor on February 17, 1864. With much effort and tension on the part of the Confederate seamen, the sub got beneath the *Housatonic*'s hull, and the crew began fastening the torpedo to it. Everything seemed to be working well when the fuse suddenly went off ahead of time. The explosion caused both the *Housatonic* and the *Hunley* to go to the bottom. Although destroyed in action, the *Hunley* is credited with being the first submarine to sink a surface ship.

Inventors in America and Europe continued their efforts to build workable submarines. By the end of the nineteenth century they were meet-

Model of the Confederate submarine Hunley. *The torpedo charge was carried at the tip of the long boom. (Division of Naval History, U.S. National Museum)*

ing with considerable success. Technological advances in the manufacture and fabrication of metals; in the creation and development of new propulsion units, such as the diesel and gasoline internal combustion engines and electric motors; in the invention of the storage battery as an electrical source; in stronger pumps and improved compressed-air devices—all played a major part in that development work.

One of the best-known submarines of the late nineteenth century was a fictional undersea boat created by the French author Jules Verne. The father of science-fiction writing, Verne developed in his mind a superbly efficient submarine to which he gave the name *Nautilus*. He then sent the craft on an imaginary adventurous undersea journey around the world, carrying Captain Nemo and his crew. Their experiences were told in Verne's book *Twenty Thousand Leagues Under the Sea,* first published in 1870. The book thrilled many readers then, and it still does today.

Jules Verne read hundreds of technical books and journals to make the background of his story sound authentic. How well he did his research and also exercised his imagination can be seen by the technical details he provides. The French writer has his characters using underwater air-breathing systems for brief walks on the ocean floor after leaving the *Nautilus.* Such apparatus was still in the earliest development stage in his time. Verne also imagined his submarine driven by electric motors for undersea travel. Electrical power units were to have a major part in the development of the first practical submarine.

In the United States the most important work leading to the successful type of submarine imagined by Jules Verne was carried out by Simon Lake and John P. Holland. Both men constructed highly successful undersea boats about the turn of the century.

Simon Lake designed and built his *Argonaut* in 1897. The following year he proved the vessel by sailing it on the open seas from Norfolk, Virginia, to New York harbor. Lake was confident that the demonstration would interest United States naval authorities to the point where they would want to make the submarine a part of the American fleet. Unsuccessful in this effort, he peddled his invention in Europe, where it found a warmer welcome.

John P. Holland began serious work on submarine designs in 1875, when he sent plans for a one-man, torpedo-carrying, undersea boat to officials of the United States Navy. His submarine was 16½ feet long and could travel submerged at a speed of 3 knots. Its stern propeller was turned by foot-operated pedals. Its torpedoes, stored behind the crewman, were to be attached to the hull of an enemy ship and fired electrically from a safe distance. The Navy was not ready for a weapon of this kind and turned the proposal down. It is interesting to note that the Japanese used a strikingly similar one-man submarine in their attack on Pearl Harbor during World War II.

Undaunted by this failure, Holland continued working with submarines until, in 1900, the United States Navy became sufficiently impressed to purchase its first underwater fighting ship.

The earliest of the Holland-built Navy submarines had a length of 54 feet, a 6-knot speed submerged, and could carry a crew of six. When traveling beneath the sea, Holland's submarine

One of the earliest of John P. Holland's successful submarines. (General Dynamics, Electric Boat Division)

was driven by electric motors powered by storage batteries. On the surface the submarine was propelled by gasoline engines.

Holland was not the only inventor who thought of adapting electric motors for propelling submarines while submerged. Others in Europe, especially in England and France, were just as active in trying to turn this visionary idea of Jules Verne's into a reality. The English-built submarine *Porpoise,* which appeared in 1896, was equipped with an electric motor, battery powered, that gave the vessel a speed of 3 knots submerged. In France the *Gymnote,* which took to the seas the same year, was also electrically driven, and it could travel at a rate of 7 knots on the surface and 5 knots beneath the water. More successful than other submarines of its day, the *Gymnote* was a steel-hulled, 60-foot giant that could travel more than 100 miles in a single trip beneath the waves.

By the time World War I broke out in 1914,

submarines had advanced technically to such a degree that they were full-time members of surface naval fleets. With larger, stronger hulls, complex ballast systems for diving and ascending, efficient dual-power units for surface and subsurface travel, and air-supply systems, submarines were capable of plunging to more than 150 feet in depth and voyaging for hundreds of miles. In the first world conflict the submarine proved itself one of the most effective naval weapons ever produced.

The addition of a snorkel made underwater fighting craft even more deadly in World War II. Then, during the postwar years in the United States, a completely revolutionary change was made in the submarine: an atomic engine was developed and harnessed to the vessel. The world's first atomic-powered submarine, the *Nautilus,* was launched in 1955. The new breed of submarines that this pioneering vessel spawned can dive far deeper than the older models and travel around the world while completely submerged. With the atomic-driven *Nautilus* the technical world had at last caught up with Jules Verne's fantasy.

Throughout the history of the submarine, it was considered primarily as a military weapon. The one exception to this, perhaps, was its brief employment for carrying cargo during wartime. Only now is this seagoing vessel being put to peaceful uses such as scientific research. For its present-day nonmilitary activities, the submarine has been transformed into a unique vessel. Before discussing these novel craft and the work they do, one other aspect of man's technical efforts to return to the undersea world must also be considered: the development of diving suits and air-breathing apparatus.

The attempts of inventors to create practical diving suits and underwater air-breathing equipment are almost as old as their efforts to build diving bells and undersea vehicles. One of the first and more productive was Leonardo da Vinci (1452–1519). A veritable genius in whatever field he turned his interests to, Da Vinci was an extraordinary inventor. He designed submarines for military purposes and a snorkel device that was far superior to the simple reed tube of ancient times. Da Vinci's snorkel consisted of a leather helmet with windows for the diver to see through while beneath the water. A long tube was connected to the helmet and reached to the surface, allowing the diver to breathe fresh air.

Another product of Da Vinci's fertile mind was swim fins to be attached to a diver's hands and feet. These permitted an underwater swimmer to travel faster and farther. Benjamin Franklin, who probably learned of Da Vinci's swim fins through books, built similar devices for himself and found that they did indeed increase one's swimming speed.

Leonardo da Vinci also designed underwater breathing equipment for divers that required no oxygen supply from a surface source. A bag of air was to be carried on the diver's chest. Finally, the Renaissance inventor proposed a leather diving suit completely enclosing the wearer, which was to be used with the self-contained breathing apparatus. This was one of the earliest attempts to create the scuba equipment so widely used by present-day underwater swimmers. (The modern term *scuba* is from the words *s*elf-*c*ontained *u*nderwater *b*reathing *a*pparatus.)

Many of Leonardo da Vinci's technical ideas

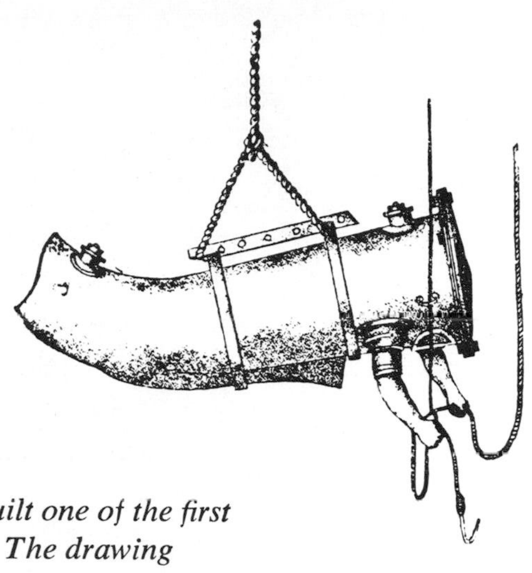

John Lethbridge of England built one of the first rigid diving chambers in 1715. The drawing above is believed to be a close approximation of his invention. (Siebe Gorman & Co., Ltd.)

were too advanced for their time and were never actually constructed. Except for his swim fins, Da Vinci's inventions for underwater swimming would have been impractical, according to modern scuba divers.

English inventors in the early 1700's developed diving suits and helmets of wood and leather with varying success. John Lethbridge made one of the more unusual such pieces of equipment in 1715. He called it a "diving engine." Lethbridge's device was made of wood and shaped like a tapered barrel. It was 6 feet long, 2½ feet in diameter at one end, and 1½ feet in diameter at the other. Two holes in the side were provided for the diver to slip his arms through. The wooden diving "dress" also had a glass porthole 4 inches in diameter so that the diver could see his underwater surroundings.

The diver crawled into this wooden suit feet first. Lying facedown, he then put his arms through the holes. A top piece was screwed into place, sealing the diver inside the unit. A strong rope

Augustus Siebe's first open diving helmet of 1819. (Siebe Gorman & Co., Ltd.)

attached to the device lowered the horizontally positioned diver into the water. Air pumped by a bellows was sent to him through a tube. According to Lethbridge, he used his wooden diver's suit many times to depths of as much as sixty feet for periods of up to half an hour.

The first truly workable diving suit and helmet dates from 1819—the invention of Augustus Siebe, a German-born inventor living in England.

Siebe's diving suit, known as the "open" type, was a waist-length jacket made of leather and canvas for strength and watertightness. The bottom portion hung loose and open. Attached to the upper part of the jacket was a globular brass helmet, with three small windows around the front, and a breastplate. The wearer looked much like a knight in armor of medieval days. Fresh air was pumped under pressure to the helmet through a pipe reaching to the surface. Excess air and the diver's exhaled air escaped through the loose, open, bottom part of the jacket.

Although it worked reasonably well, Siebe's diving suit had one serious fault. It worked on the same principle as the open diving bell. The diver using it had to be careful to remain in a perfectly upright position while walking underwater. If he were to trip and fall, the air within the suit would escape and be quickly replaced with water. Needless to say, this was extremely hazardous, if not fatal, for the diver.

Eighteen years later Siebe improved on his original invention by making a closed suit that completely sealed the diver in a watertight covering. Special valves were designed to let bad air escape while preventing water from entering the suit. Siebe added still another valve that permitted the diver to control his incoming air supply.

Siebe's pioneering diving suit was basically the same design as that in use today by so-called "hard hat" divers. They are called this because of the metal helmets they wear. Modern suits are made of canvas and rubber, with tight rubber seals at the diver's wrists and ankles. The metal helmet and breastplate are also much like the ones designed by Siebe, with round windows at the sides and front. Heavy lead weights are fastened around the diver's waist and also to the bottom of his shoes. These are helpful when he makes his descent and aid him in keeping his equilibrium while on the bottom of the sea.

An air hose, a strong rope, and a telephone line link the modern diver with his colleagues on the surface. The air supply used is often a mixture of nitrogen and oxygen or helium and oxygen. The

Modern hard-hat diving gear. (Siebe Gorman & Co., Ltd.)

rope or "lifeline" serves as a communication link, if no telephone is used, and also as a means of hauling the diver to the surface.

For more than a hundred years the Siebe-type diving suit has been valuable for such underwater tasks as working on bridge foundations, salvaging treasure from sunken ships, and helping to raise ships and submarines that have gone to the bottom. The average depth at which divers using Siebe equipment work is 200 feet. They can carry on their activities at this level for three or four hours. For brief emergency dives, hard-hat aquanauts can plunge more than 500 feet.

Although extremely important for underwater work, hard-hat diving gear has its limitations. The diver is restricted in his movements on the sea floor by his air hose and other connections with a surface ship. The closed diving suit is also bulky and, despite the buoyancy action of the water, further limits a diver's underwater freedom. The more recently developed scuba has given divers a vastly more convenient type of underwater equipment.

The self-contained underwater breathing apparatus, so popular with present-day divers, can trace a good part of its ancestry back to 1825, when William H. James of England designed underwater breathing equipment that used compressed air. The air supply was contained in a cylindrical iron belt that the diver wore around his waist. The inventor claimed that a diver using this self-contained breathing apparatus could remain on the floor of the sea for as long as one hour.

A much-improved model, and one to which modern scuba is more closely related, was developed in 1865 by Benoît Rouquayrol and Auguste Denayrouze, two Frenchmen. The device they created consisted of a metal cylinder of air that the diver wore on his back. A tube led from

This is considered the first self-contained diving suit. It was designed by William H. James in 1825. A cast-iron belt around the diver's waist held a supply of compressed air. (Siebe Gorman & Co., Ltd.)

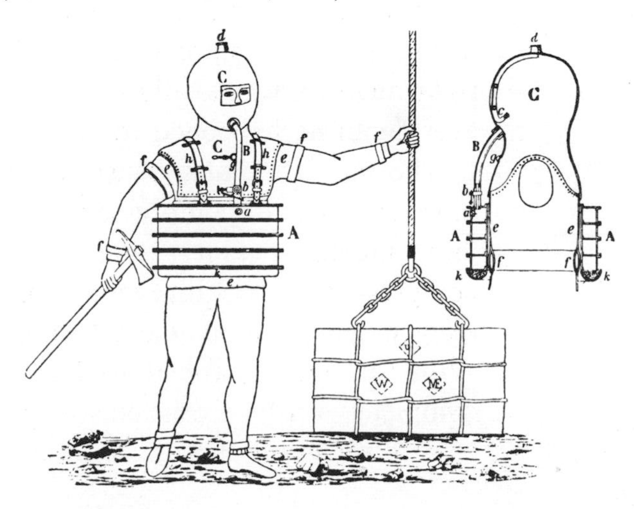

the cylinder to a mouthpiece. A regulating valve on the tube controlled the amount of air breathed. Air was pumped into the cylinder from a surface source, although the hose could be completely disconnected to give the diver more freedom of movement. When the hose was disconnected, a diver's endurance was then limited by the amount of air held in the cylinder.

Primitive, perhaps, when compared to the equipment now in use, the Rouquayrol-Denayrouze underwater breathing unit did have some advantages over hard-hat diving gear. Most important of these was the freedom of movement it allowed underwater swimmers. Two years after it was created, the Frenchmen's diving equipment was put into commercial production. Not long afterward it was in considerable use throughout Europe.

The scuba now in use was created by Jacques-Yves Cousteau, world-renowned French oceanographer, and Émile Gagnan, a fellow countryman and engineer. Their self-contained underwater breathing apparatus was successfully tested in 1943. The most advanced part in the new equipment was an automatic valve. The valve regulated the supply of compressed air to insure that the right quantity was available to the diver at whatever depth he happened to be.

The modern scuba consists mainly of two or more cylinders of compressed air, a regulating device, breathing tubes, and a mouthpiece. The compressed-air mixture may be pure oxygen, oxygen-helium, or oxygen, helium, and nitrogen. With this unit strapped to his back, a diver is completely on his own beneath the waves.

A diver's air supply contains the same substances that we breathe in the air on land, but in different proportions. Ordinary air at sea level is almost 79 percent nitrogen and 21 percent oxygen. Also present in the air are small quantities of argon and carbon dioxide and traces, too, of xenon, helium, hydrogen, and other gases.

A special breathing-gas mixture is used by divers to reduce the danger of "bends" or decompression sickness. The increased pressure at an underwater depth makes some of the nitrogen in the air the diver breathes dissolve in his blood. If he rises to the surface too quickly, he is exposed to a rapidly falling outside pressure that causes nitrogen in his system to form bubbles in the bloodstream. These bubbles concentrate at the joints and in the bone marrow. This is extremely painful and immobilizes the victim. The bubbles may also block circulation to vital organs and bring on death. To readjust his body to normal air pressure so that he avoids the bends, a diver must undergo slow decompression inside a pressurized chamber.

Breathing nitrogen can also cause nitrogen narcosis or "rapture of the deep." Divers in this state feel intoxicated and behave erratically.

To reduce the danger of the bends and nitrogen narcosis, various breathing-gas mixtures containing only small quantities of nitrogen have been sought and developed. One of the first to come into existence was a combination of hydrogen and oxygen. However, this too was abandoned, because of the explosive nature of hydrogen. A helium-oxygen mixture was then created that has met with considerable success and is widely used.

Despite the creation of better gas mixtures for diving, the bends remain a danger after long sub-

Front and back views of a diver wearing a Mark VI semiclosed mixed-gas scuba. (U.S. Navy)

mergence. Divers must still undergo the slow process of decompression to insure their safety.

The average depth at which scuba divers operate is close to 200 feet. Current developments with new safe breathing mixtures and diving gear are expected to increase their range to more than 1,000 feet in the not-too-distant future.

Actually, there are three different versions of scuba: open (Cousteau-Gagnan type), closed, and semiclosed. With the open model the diver's exhaled air passes directly into the sea. When his supply of compressed air is used up he must return to the surface. The closed type of scuba does not permit the escape of exhaled air. The air is repurified (carbon dioxide is removed) by being passed through a chemical, such as lithium hydroxide, within a canister. This permits the breathing air to be used over and over by the diver. The semi-closed model has a special relief valve for the escape of a certain amount of exhaled gas into the water. The diver may adjust this valve manually. The amount of gas permitted to escape helps regulate the diver's buoyancy.

The open type of scuba is considered the safest and is the most widely used. The closed and semi-closed models are recent developments and permit the diver to remain on the sea floor for longer periods.

Modern scuba has made it possible for man to swim underwater with almost the ease of fish. Perhaps more than any other piece of diving equipment it has brought him closer to his sea heritage. The combination of undersea chambers, deep-diving submersibles, and scuba has made accessible to man an underwater world every bit as exciting and as filled with promise for mankind's benefit as the world of outer space.

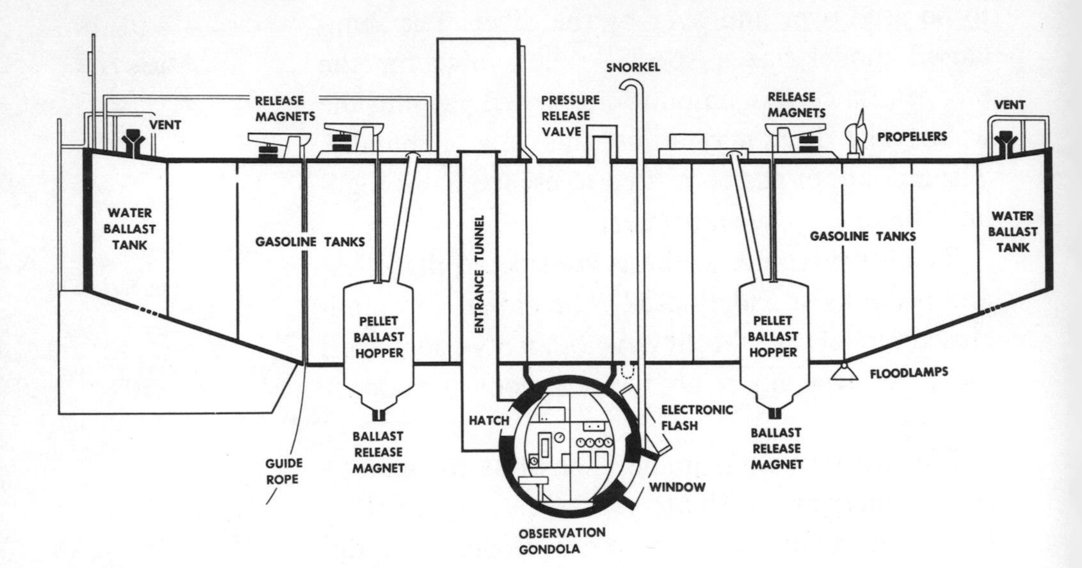

Diagram of the Trieste. *(U.S. Navy)*

Chapter 2
Diving for science

Dr. William Beebe, American naturalist and explorer, was the first to demonstrate the value of the deep-diving vehicle for scientific work. Between 1931 and 1934 he made extraordinary dives in a bathysphere to depths of more than 3,000 feet. This closed underwater chamber was created by Dr. Beebe and Otis Barton. A globe-shaped steel structure with walls one and a half inches thick, it was lowered and raised by means of a steel cable and winch from the deck of a surface ship. Dr. Beebe's daring plunges into an underwater world deeper than any ever seen by man before resulted in many important discoveries. His diving exploits were not to be equaled or surpassed until 1953, when Dr. Auguste Piccard invented the bathyscaphe *Trieste*. The bathyscaphe is a boatlike vehicle capable of diving to the deepest parts of the ocean and moving around under its own power. The word comes from the Greek *bathos* (deep) and *scaphos* (boat).

It is generally agreed by oceanographers that Dr. Piccard's *Trieste* was the real beginning of the current exploration and study of the undersea world.

Dr. Piccard worked out many of the basic features of the *Trieste* with an earlier model, the FNRS-2. The *Trieste* has two main parts: a long, horizontal buoyancy chamber and a spherical crew chamber beneath it. The buoyancy chamber is about 50 feet long and has a diameter of 11½ feet.

The interior of the buoyancy chamber is divided into twelve compartments. Ten of these contain more than 34,000 gallons of gasoline; the remaining two on either end are filled with seawater when the *Trieste* descends into the ocean. In addition, two cylindrical tanks or hoppers are placed fore and aft within the chamber. These carry ten tons of iron pellets. The gasoline, seawater, and iron pellets are all part of a unique ballast and buoyancy control system devised by Dr. Piccard to take the *Trieste* to the deepest spots in the ocean and back to the surface again. Gasoline was chosen because it is lighter and more compressible than seawater.

Because the strong pressure forces are equalized by fluids both inside and outside the buoyancy chamber at extreme depths, its walls are constructed of thin steel plates.

The crew compartment, or gondola, is located beneath the center of the buoyancy chamber. It is a ball 6 feet in diameter, made of high-strength steel. The shape was deliberately chosen because a sphere offers the greatest structural strength for resisting the crushing water pressure at extreme depths. A porthole of strong plexiglass on the lower side of the sphere enables the two-man crew to observe the undersea world. Entrance into the observation compartment is by way of a vertical tunnel extending from a conning tower on the *Trieste*'s deck down through the buoyancy chamber. The tunnel connects to a hatch on the side of the compartment.

The deep-diving submersible Trieste *about to be lowered into the sea. The sphere at the bottom is the crew compartment. (U.S. Navy)*

The *Trieste* is equipped with five electric motors located along the top of the buoyancy chamber. Sealed in oil-filled compartments, each motor has a capacity of 2 horsepower. The motors give this pioneering underwater vehicle a speed of 1 knot and allow it to maneuver vertically, horizontally, or at an angle. The motors are driven by batteries inside the crew chamber.

The *Trieste* carries a variety of equipment. This includes oxygen bottles, containers of chemicals for cleaning used air, an echo sounder, movie and still cameras, searchlights, closed-circuit television, a device for measuring vertical and horizontal speeds, current meters, plankton samplers, and automatic water-sampling bottles.

All these devices and tools help oceanographers to operate undersea vehicles and to conduct research. The echo sounder tells the oceanographer the depth of the ocean around him. It sends out sound pulses. The pulses or waves hit the sea bottom or underwater objects and bounce back. The time it takes the echo to return is measured by sensitive receiving equipment aboard the vessel. This time is computed with the known speed of sound in water to calculate the distance to the bottom of the sea at that point. Modern echo sounders are so sensitive they can detect shipwrecks and schools of fish. The equipment replaces the older technique of throwing a weighted line into the sea.

Closed-circuit television permits observers on the surface to see simultaneously with the submersible's crew the underwater scenes being taken by the vehicle's television cameras. Reception is "closed" to anyone else.

When diving the *Trieste* has no physical connection with a surface ship. The submersible is completely free to move around, just as easily as a submarine. Telephone and television communication are the only links between the *Trieste* crew and colleagues on a mother ship above.

Famous for his balloon flights into the stratosphere back in the 1930's, Dr. Piccard, a Swiss physicist, applied the principles of balloon construction and flight to the development of his bathyscaphe, the *Trieste.* Its elongated body or buoyancy chamber can be compared to the gas-filled section of a balloon; the small, spherical chamber located midway beneath the body is much like the gondola that hangs beneath the gas-filled bag of the balloon.

Underwater descents begin when the two end compartments and the entrance tunnel are flooded with water. This ballast, together with the weight of the gasoline and the iron pellets, takes the *Trieste* downward. If the crew wishes to hold the vehicle at a certain level, a measured amount of gasoline or shot ballast is released. The *Trieste* then remains suspended in its watery world, neutrally buoyant, like a gas-filled balloon tethered to a rope.

After completing an underwater assignment, the crew returns to the surface by releasing all the iron shot-ballast. Free of the excess weight and now in a state of positive buoyancy, the *Trieste* ascends like a balloon headed for the stratosphere.

Built in Trieste, Italy, Dr. Piccard's bathyscaphe was launched in August 1953. The vehicle's first dive was limited to a cautious 26 feet beneath the Mediterranean Sea. The *Trieste* proved itself the following month by reaching a depth of 10,300 feet. A series of successful dives followed.

The greatest undersea accomplishment of the *Trieste* took place on January 23, 1960. That day Dr. Jacques Piccard (son of Dr. Auguste Piccard) and Navy Lieutenant Donald Walsh took the submersible down to the astonishing depth of 35,800 feet. Project Nekton, as this hazardous plunge was called, took place in the Challenger Deep (the Mariana Trench) off the island of Guam. This is close to the greatest ocean depth so far known, 36,198 feet, also in the Mariana Trench. The record depth was discovered in 1957 by oceanographers aboard the Russian survey ship *Vityaz*.

The ocean bottom has features much the same as those on land. There are numerous hills and terraces, vast level stretches, and enormous mountain ranges. A great many peaks of these mountains are higher than Mt. Everest. Where they stick out above the ocean surface, islands are formed. The Mid-Atlantic Ridge is the largest of these sea-bottom chains of mountains. Canyons exist in the ocean floor too, similar to the Grand Canyon. Called trenches in the ocean world, these are long, narrow, immensely deep depressions. The sides of the trenches are generally steep. A relatively small area of a trench may be its deepest part. This is called a deep, usually with a prefix name for its discoverer. The Cook Deep, for example, is named for the famous British explorer and navigator Captain James Cook.

By means of Project Nekton Lieutenant Walsh and Jacques Piccard hoped to answer a question that marine scientists had long wondered about. Did animal life exist in the deepest parts of the oceans? There was some doubt that life was possible there because of the enormous water pressure and the complete absence of sunlight.

Sunlight commonly penetrates the ocean to a depth of about 300 feet, and faint traces of light have been detected as deep as 2,000 feet. It is in the sunlit regions of the ocean that all plant life flourishes and most of the fish exist.

A cutaway chart of undersea regions. (Columbus Laboratories, Battelle Memorial Institute)

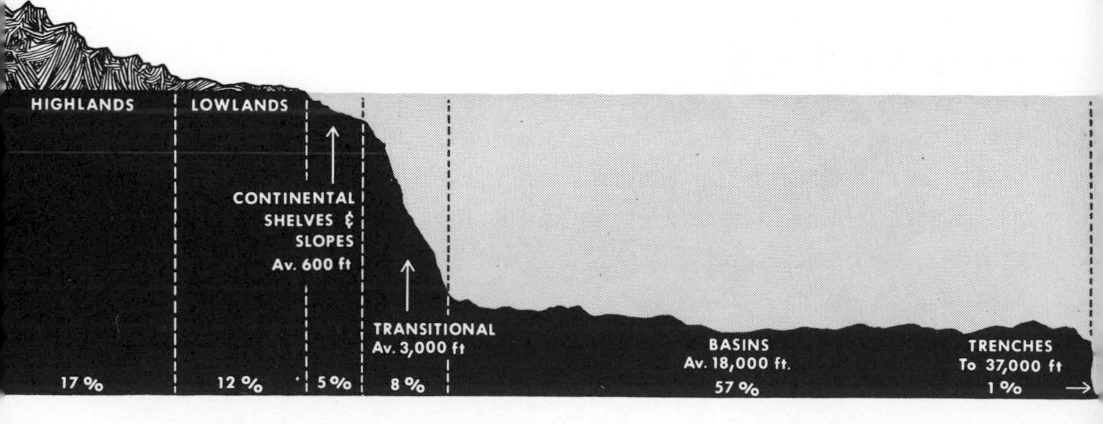

It took the daring oceanographers in *Trieste* four hours and forty-eight minutes to reach the floor of the Challenger Deep. In the cold, inky darkness of this mysterious undersea world, they switched on the powerful searchlights. To their surprise, they saw marine life moving about within the revealing rays. One species was described as flat, about a foot in length, and looking much like the common halibut or fluke. Another creature had a shrimplike appearance.

After remaining for twenty minutes at their record-breaking depth, the two oceanographers released ballast and started slowly upward. Traveling more than six miles vertically, their submersible broke the surface of the sea after three hours and seventeen minutes. Throughout their historic underwater journey, the crew of the *Trieste* remained in touch with colleagues aboard a tender ship by means of a sonar communication system. This involves sending sound signals underwater from one point to another. The transmission pattern of the signals can be translated into a voice or coded form of communication.

In 1958 the *Trieste* was acquired by the United States Navy and turned over to the Naval Electronics Laboratory Center at San Diego, California. After short use, naval engineers saw that the *Trieste* could be improved upon. The thin walls of the buoyancy float were so weak that towing the craft through only a moderately rough sea was hazardous. When the alteration work was completed, the *Trieste*'s float chamber had been made longer and stronger. In the course of reconstruction the crew chamber was repositioned so that it was partially enclosed in the float above.

Despite the changes, the *Trieste* still resembled

After the U.S. Navy's redesign work the bathyscaphe Trieste *had a somewhat different appearance.*
(U.S. Navy)

the original vehicle Dr. Piccard had built. Now there was less danger of damaging the craft in choppy seas, it was more maneuverable, and it could travel farther while submerged. This improved vehicle was identified as the *Trieste II*.

In June 1963 the *Trieste II* was called upon to perform a mission outside its usual scientific activities. The United States Navy employed it to search for the nuclear submarine *Thresher,* which had failed to return from a test dive in April of that year. The submarine had gone on a trial cruise about 200 miles east of Boston and was believed to have met disaster in the cold, grey waters of the Atlantic Ocean at a depth of more than 8,000 feet. Surface rescue vessels searched in vain for the stricken submarine.

The *Trieste II* was brought from its base in California to see what it could do. On its third dive remains of the crushed *Thresher* were spotted.

Later, with the use of its mechanical arm, the undersea vehicle picked up and brought to the surface a length of pipe that was identified as being part of the *Thresher*'s galley. The *Scorpion,* another of the Navy's deep-diving submarines, was lost in May 1968.

Now, a basic characteristic of water pressure is that it becomes greater with depth. At sea level the air presses on our bodies at 14.7 pounds per square inch. Scientists call this amount of pressure one atmosphere. In the sea, water pressure increases one atmosphere for every 33 feet of depth. In the deepest parts of the ocean, over 30,000 feet, the pressure is nearly seven tons per square inch. This is almost a thousand times the atmospheric pressure existing on the earth's surface.

As an example of what this pressure can do, a block of wood at 3,000 feet down will be squeezed by a force of 8,100 pounds per square inch to a point where it will be reduced to half its original volume and will sink still farther. At 20,000 feet

Trieste II *played an important part in finding the sunken nuclear submarine* Thresher. *Here the submersible is being towed to the search area, 220 miles east of Boston. (U.S. Navy)*

A portion of the wrecked nuclear submarine Thresher *photographed by the* Trieste II. *(U.S. Navy)*

down air will be squeezed so compactly that it will weigh as much as the surrounding water. Little wonder then that even though they are especially constructed for strength, nuclear submarines such as the *Thresher,* plunging out of control to depths far beyond their limits, are crushed like eggshells. It is this enormous pressure at great depths that limits the downward range of human divers.

Since it first took to the water in 1953, the *Trieste* has more than proved its abilities and usefulness. It demonstrated that scientists could use undersea vehicles of its type to broaden their knowledge of the ocean depths, about which so little is known.

The *Trieste*'s activities soon stimulated the production of a whole family of underwater vehicles. Among these is the Diving Saucer SP-300, *Soucoupe Sous-Marin,* which has become as well known as the *Trieste.*

The Diving Saucer is the brainchild of the world-famous underwater explorer Jacques-Yves

Cousteau. He began thinking of his undersea vehicle as far back as 1951, and six years later he completed the first model. Unfortunately, a cable broke while the vehicle was being put through a series of unmanned test dives, and it plunged more than 3,000 feet to the sea bottom. Although the loss was painful, Cousteau was confident that the vehicle's basic design was sound and he proceeded to build a second. This has proved enormously successful, taking Cousteau and his colleagues on hundreds of voyages beneath the sea.

The core of the Diving Saucer is a horizontal, ellipse-shaped hull made of two "shells" of ¾-inch-thick, high-strength steel welded together at the edges. This hull is enclosed in a fiberglass covering. The submersible is aptly named; it really does look something like a giant saucer. This streamlined shape permits it to move easily through the water. Airplanes are streamlined for the same reason: so they may speed through the air with the least amount of resistance. With its fiberglass shroud, the Diving Saucer has a diameter of 9½

Jacques-Yves Cousteau's Diving Saucer undergoing final inspection before entering the undersea world. (Westinghouse Underseas Division)

feet and a height of 5 feet. It weighs close to 7,000 pounds and has room for a crew of two.

The Diving Saucer's propulsion system is one of its more interesting features. Rather than conventional propellers, jet nozzles squirting streams of water under pressure are used to drive the undersea vehicle.

The two plastic jet nozzles, bent at right angles, are positioned on the right and left sides of the Diving Saucer. These nozzles or hydrojets can be turned 360 degrees. Thus, depending on their angle, the jets can drive the undersea vehicle forward, backward, up, or down, and even spin it around a fixed point like a top. An electrically driven pump forces the seawater under pressure through small openings and out of the nozzles. The pump gets its power from batteries carried on the outer surface of the steel hull. The Diving Saucer's hydrojets can propel it at a cruising speed of 1 knot and a maximum speed of 1½ knots.

The two-man crew of Cousteau's underwater vehicle, a pilot and observer, lie facedown on rubber couches. Because it is a strain to keep one's head in an upright position while lying down, chin rests are provided. The vehicle's life-support system consists of a breathing-gas mixture maintained at the pressure equivalent to that existing on the earth's surface. Air-purifying chemicals that cleanse the used air and allow it to be recirculated are also part of the system. The Diving Saucer's life-support system permits the crew to carry on its underwater explorations for a period of twenty-four hours. Generally, dives are limited to four hours.

Crew members look through two viewing ports made of strong plexiglass. Three additional wide-angle ports are located in the top of the hull. Two other ports are used for shooting movie and still pictures of the underwater world. Seachlights on the outside of the vehicle light up the area being observed.

The inner surface of the crew's compartment is almost entirely covered with instruments and switches. These items include such things as meters to show air pressure and carbon dioxide percentage within the cabin, a gyrocompass for determining the direction of travel, a depth gauge and echo sounders that reveal the nearness of the ocean bottom, and indicators showing the trim position of the vehicle. Tape recorders are used to make voice records of the crew's observations. Instead of making notes their hands are kept free to do such chores as piloting the vehicle or operating cameras and other equipment.

The Diving Saucer has a mechanical arm attached to its forward side. The arm is controlled by the crew from within the cabin. It is extremely agile at picking up marine specimens and placing

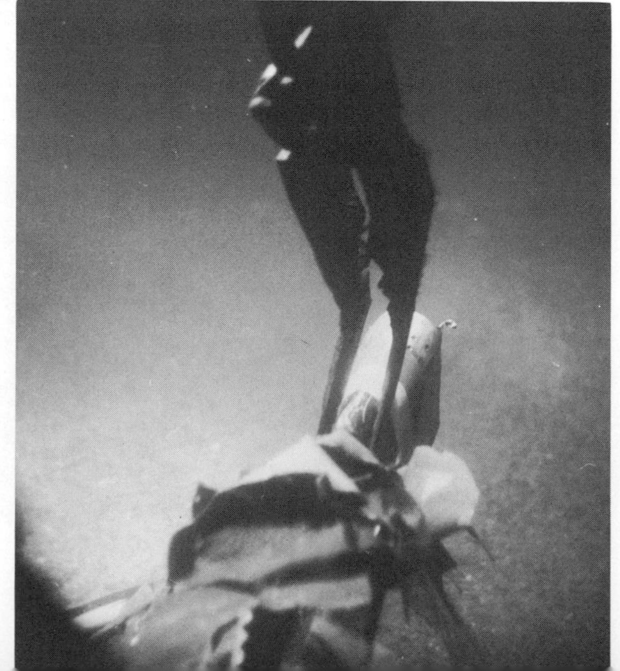

The view from inside a submersible showing a mechanical arm picking up debris from a wreck. This is the arm of a Japanese vehicle, the Yomiuri. *(The Yomiuri Shimbun, Japan)*

them in a basket beneath the saucer's viewing ports.

A simple but ingenious ballast system gives the crew precise control over the vehicle's dives, ascents, and neutral buoyancy position. When the Diving Saucer is ready to plunge to the sea bottom, it starts with two 55-pound weights of pig iron. If the crew wishes to slow its rate of descent, one of the weights is released. To rise to the surface again, both weights are dropped off. Also, to help attain neutral buoyancy at a particular depth—precision trimming, as it is called—a ballast tank within the pressure hull can be flooded with or emptied of seawater. In an emergency, when a quick ascent is needed, a weight of almost 600 pounds carried beneath the Diving Saucer can be released.

Like a twin-eyed monster of the ocean depths, the Diving Saucer moves serenely over the coral-covered sea floor. (Westinghouse Underseas Division)

A mercury balance arrangement adds greatly to the Diving Saucer's underwater maneuvering ability. This system has forward and aft tanks. One hundred and sixty-five pounds of mercury can be pumped from one tank to the other, tilting the vehicle in an upward or downward position. Cousteau designed his underwater vehicle to have a maximum diving range of 1,000 feet. Its main underwater assignments are confined to the continental shelves. These regions extend from the waterline of land masses and islands seaward for an average distance of 40 miles. In some world areas they may range from almost no width to several hundred miles. From the edges of the shelves the land drops sharply downward to become the continental slopes.

The Diving Saucer was first successfully tested in 1959 in the warm, clear waters off Puerto Rico. After that, countless other voyages to the bottom of the Caribbean, Mediterranean, and Red seas were achieved. In 1964 the submersible was loaned to the United States Navy for research conducted by members of the Scripps Institution of Oceanography at La Jolla, California. The vehicle made geological studies of two sea canyons 900 feet beneath the Pacific off La Jolla.

More recently Cousteau took the Diving Saucer and a sister craft on an expedition to Bolivia for exploring the depths of sky-high Lake Titicaca. Nestled among the towering slopes of the Andes Mountains, Lake Titicaca has long been a mystery to scientists and local people. Legend stated that the lake was bottomless and that in some sections its water hid fabulous gold treasure of past civilizations. The Cousteau expedition found no treasure. But it did determine that Lake Titicaca, like

The Alvin *being readied for launching. (Woods Hole Oceanographic Institution)*

all lakes, had a bottom—a little more than 700 feet from the surface.

The highly successful Diving Saucer led to the design and construction of a similar midget submersible, the *Alvin*. The United States Navy sponsored its development, then turned it over to scientists of the Woods Hole Oceanographic Institution, in Massachusetts. This is one of the oldest and most highly respected marine laboratories in America.

The *Alvin,* named for Allyn Collins Vine, an oceanographer at Woods Hole, was built exclusively for deep-diving research work. Cousteau had believed and proved with his Diving Saucer that small submersibles of this type are the best means for carrying scientists, safely and comfortably, to the ocean bottom for their complex undersea studies.

The *Alvin* is a short, snub-nosed vehicle 23 feet long and with an 8-foot beam. The real heart of the vehicle is a pressure sphere 7 feet in diameter made of high-strength steel more than 1¼ inches thick. This is the crew compartment, large enough for three men: a pilot and two observers. The *Alvin* can dive to a depth of 6,000 feet. The

Alvin's life-support system is similar to that of the Diving Saucer's and can operate for twenty-four hours to sustain the crew.

Four viewing ports, at the front and beneath the body of the vehicle, give the crew a wide range for observing the underwater environment. Crew members enter the *Alvin* through a hatch at the top of the sphere. Power for operating the submersible's equipment comes from storage batteries fixed to the outside of the sphere but within the streamlined outer hull. In the event of an emergency, when there would bc need to rise to the surface quickly, the heavy batteries could be easily released.

The chubby *Alvin* is equipped with three propellers. Two are located on either side of the vehicle and are called lift propellers. They are used for driving the submersible up, down, forward, or backward. A third and larger propeller is fixed to the stern. It can be turned from side to side to steer the *Alvin* to the right or left. This is similar to the way an outboard motor is turned to steer a small surface boat.

A diagram showing the details of Alvin*'s construction and operating equipment. (Woods Hole Oceanographic Institution)*

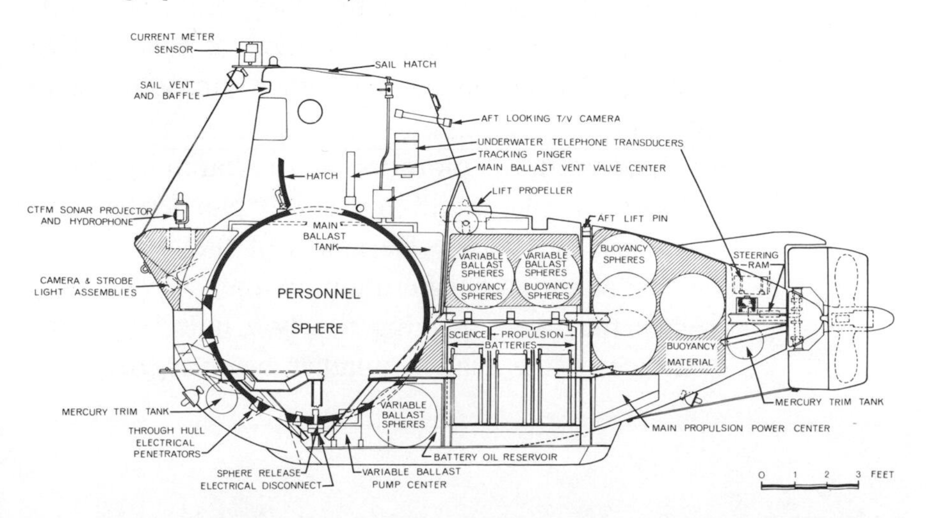

The two lift propellers can be operated individually for even greater maneuverability. By reversing one propeller while operating the other in a forward direction, the *Alvin* can be made to turn on its own axis, like a revolving door. All the propellers are driven by reversible hydraulic motors. The basic source of power, however, is provided by electric motors encased in oil-filled compartments.

The *Alvin* has a control system that permits the pilot to tilt it at about a 20-degree angle upward or downward. This is accomplished by means of three spherical trim tanks, two near the bow and one in the stern. The tanks are filled half with mercury and half with oil. The liquids do not mix but remain separated; mercury, the heavier, occupies the bottom half of the tanks. A system of pipes connects the tops and bottoms of all three tanks. As the oil is pumped from the top of one tank into the top of a second tank, mercury from the second tank is forced out of the bottom and into the bottom of the first tank. By this means the weights of the three trim tanks can be increased or decreased, thus changing the fore and aft angle of the vessel.

The scientific equipment carried aboard the *Alvin* varies according to the particular research project it is being used for. Generally, however, this equipment is nearly the same as that carried by the Diving Saucer and other submersibles of its kind.

Underwater exploration and research by means of submersibles is still in the early pioneering stage and still hazardous. Designers of the *Alvin* have given careful consideration to the crew's safety when they are voyaging nearly a mile below the surface of the sea. A number of emergency fea-

A specially designed mother ship, the Lulu, *takes care of the* Alvin *when the small submersible is on an expedition. (Woods Hole Oceanographic Institution)*

tures have been built into the vehicle. For example, to give the vehicle quick, needed buoyancy for rising, explosive valves are provided which, when fired, dump the heavy mercury portion of its trim system. The *Alvin*'s mechanical arm may also be disengaged in the event it becomes hopelessly entangled with an underwater object. As a last escape measure, the spherical crew compartment can be disconnected by mechanical means from the streamlined outer shell. Since the ball-shaped chamber is positively buoyant, it will always bob to the surface under normal conditions.

On underwater scientific missions the *Alvin* is accompanied by a mother ship. This specially designed ship can lift the submersible out of the water to repair it, to recharge its batteries, and to replenish its air tanks. Also it is the surface communications center when the *Alvin* is submerged.

The *Alvin* had hardly acquired its sea legs in

1965 when it was enlisted by the United States Navy to carry out an emergency search mission. The object sought was a hydrogen bomb that had fallen into the sea off Palomares, Spain, following a midair collision of two United States Air Force planes. Only the general area where the bomb was dropped was known, and all of that area lay in deep water. After nearly three months of fruitless searching by surface ships, the *Alvin* was brought to the scene along with another deep-diving submersible, the *Aluminaut*. It was the *Alvin*'s crew that finally spotted the horrendous weapon perched precariously on an underwater ledge 2,800 feet below the surface of the sea.

The salvage efforts that followed were a hair-raising drama. One miscalculation or false move could have knocked the H-bomb off the ledge into deeper water, possibly spilling its deadly contents out and poisoning the Mediterranean Sea over a vast area for many years. By means of a special Navy-developed underwater recovery apparatus, lifting lines were successfully attached to the H-bomb, bringing it undamaged to the surface.

The *Alvin* suffered a mishap of its own in October 1968. While it was being prepared for an undersea voyage, the steel lifting cable snapped, dumping the vehicle with its hatch still open into the sea. After several unsuccessful attempts the *Alvin* was raised from its 5,000-foot resting place on the floor of the Atlantic in August 1969. The *Aluminaut* and the United States Navy Research ship *Mizar* helped with the recovery.

Not all the present family of deep submersibles are as small as the *Alvin*, or Diving Saucer. The *Aluminaut* is one of a larger breed that first made its appearance in September 1964. Forerunners

The Aluminaut, *one of the larger research submersibles, about to be launched. (General Dynamics, Electric Boat Division)*

of this ship included the *Archimedes* and the *Auguste Piccard*. Size is not the only feature that sets the *Aluminaut* apart from other submersibles. The material of which it is made is aluminum, rather than the usual high-strength steel. Looking more like a conventional submarine than many of the other present-day undersea research vehicles, the *Aluminaut* has a length of 51 feet and a diameter of 8 feet. Its hull is constructed of eleven forged aluminum sections, each 6½ inches thick. The vessel's fore and aft ends are hemispherical in shape. The hull has sufficient strength to permit the *Aluminaut* to dive to the remarkable depth of 15,000 feet. For underwater voyaging this research submersible can cruise at slightly more than 3 knots.

On normal research voyages the *Aluminaut* carries a crew of three. If necessary, the crew can be increased to as many as eight members. The entryway is at the stern of the vehicle through a raised conning tower. Beneath the conning tower and behind the stern end is a winglike structure.

The *Aluminaut* is equipped with three propellers. One is placed vertically on the top deck and

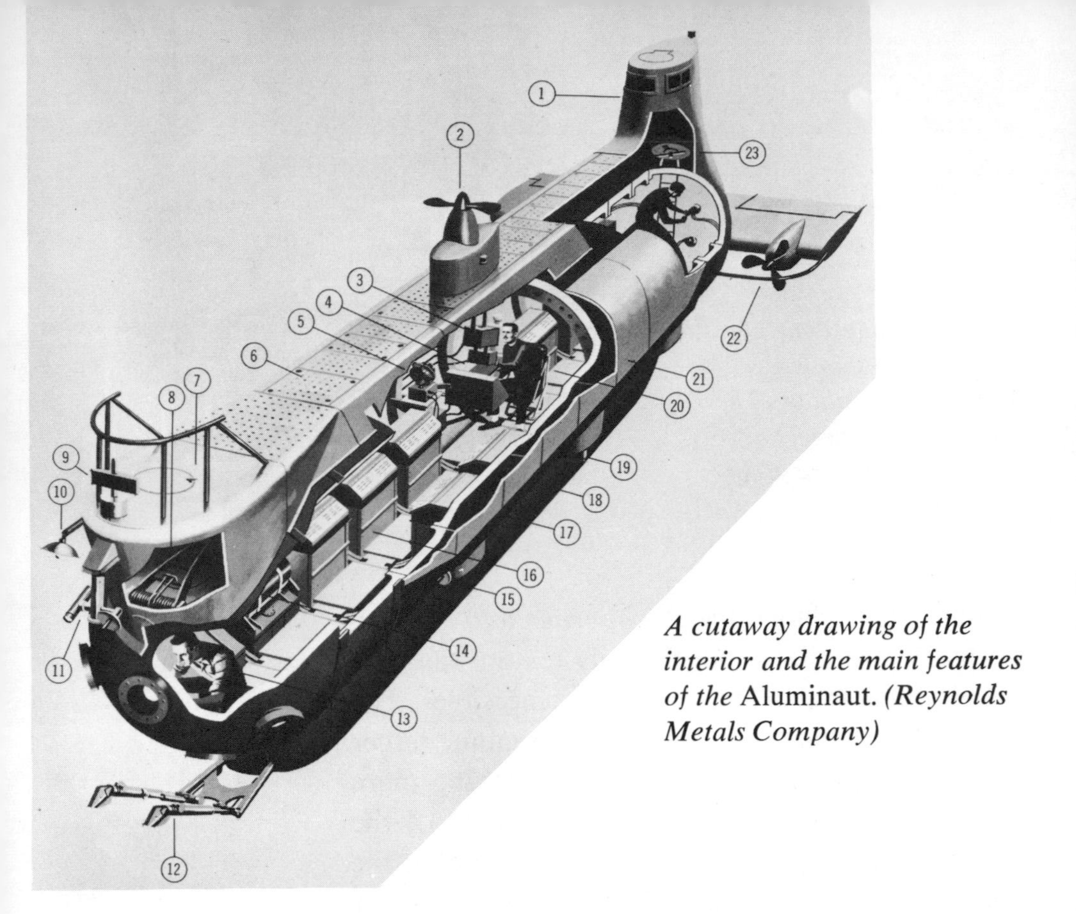

A cutaway drawing of the interior and the main features of the Aluminaut. *(Reynolds Metals Company)*

1. STERN ACCESS TRUNK
2. VERTICAL PROPULSION MOTOR
3. T.V. MONITOR
4. FORWARD SONAR DISPLAY
5. GYROCOMPASS
6. DECK SUPERSTRUCTURE
7. BOW ACCESS TRUNK
8. BOW ACCESS HATCH
9. SCANNING C.T.F.M. SONAR
10. EXTENSIBLE ILLUMINATOR
11. T.V. CAMERA & ILLUMINATOR
12. MANIPULATOR DEVICE
13. OBSERVER
14. OXYGEN FLASK
15. PORT ILLUMINATOR
16. BATTERY
17. SIDE-LOOKING SONAR (UNDER BALLAST TANK)
18. KEEL SUPERSTRUCTURE
19. SHOT BALLAST SOLENOID
20. SKIPPER
21. BALLAST TANK
22. PORT PROPULSION MOTOR
23. STERN ACCESS HATCH

is used for the submersible's up-and-down movements. Two other propellers are located at each end of the winglike structure behind the stern. These move the vehicle in a forward direction. Behind the propellers are movable rudders that help control up-and-down maneuvers. The motors driving the *Aluminaut,* one for each propeller, are battery powered. The batteries are carried within the ship. They can provide enough continuous energy for the undersea research vehicle to cruise submerged for thirty-two hours and a distance of 80 miles.

The regular life-support system carried by the *Aluminaut* can keep a crew of three alive for thirty-six hours. If an emergency occurs extra supplies of air can be piped into the system for an additional thirty-six hours. Also in the event of an emergency, the submersible's lead bar on the underside of the hull, and shot ballast, each over two tons in weight, can be dropped quickly. Should the radio equipment fail when the submersible is in trouble, a rocket and buoy device can be shot to the surface to reveal its position.

The *Aluminaut* is controlled from a station amidships, where the pilot has the usual instruments and gauges, and a monitoring television screen, to help him navigate.

The forward part of the *Aluminaut* has been arranged for the use of a scientist-observer. It contains four portholes that allow the viewer to see in front and below the bow. If the scientist spots an interesting geological or marine specimen that he would like to study at close hand, he operates two mechanical arms for retrieving it. The *Aluminaut*'s mechanical arms are nine feet long and can lift samples weighing up to 600 pounds. The samples are placed in a storage basket until the submersible returns to the surface.

Like some creature of the deep, the Aluminaut *explores the ocean floor. (Reynolds Metals Company)*

The *Aluminaut* has an impressive record of accomplishments since it first began its deep-water missions. Foremost, perhaps, was the major role it played in locating the missing H-bomb off the coast of Spain in 1966. Other more scientific events in the life of the *Aluminaut* include a test dive to 6,250 feet in the Straits of Florida, a record for undersea vehicles of its type. However, this is still far from the maximum depth of close to three miles that the *Aluminaut* was designed to reach. On another occasion the *Aluminaut* carried a group of eight scientists on a voyage beneath the Gulf Stream. In the course of the journey 1,000 feet below sea level a large area of phosphatic limestone was discovered. If this substance were mined and brought to the surface it could be processed into valuable fertilizer. Also discovered was a bone yard—the fossil remains of dugongs, whale-like relatives of sea cows. These bones were estimated to be about 25 million years old. The *Aluminaut*'s mechanical arms were used to recover several hundred pounds of the fossil specimens for laboratory study.

The *Aluminaut* has since been joined by other large undersea research vehicles, like the PX-15. This submersible is the brainchild of Jacques Piccard, the well-known oceanographer who had helped his father, Dr. Auguste Piccard, to develop the *Trieste*. It was also his idea to use the PX-15 in a unique research voyage, drifting below the surface and within the Gulf Stream current.

A warm river within an ocean, the Gulf Stream was first discovered and reported by Ponce de Leon in 1513. One of the earliest scientific investigators of the Gulf Stream was Benjamin Franklin, for whom the PX-15 has been named. It was

Franklin who had the first chart of the Gulf Stream drawn in 1769.

The Gulf Stream is formed by the joining of the North and South Equatorial currents east of the West Indies. The new current thus formed continues westward through the passages separating the Windward Islands and flows into the Caribbean Sea. Here the current piles up as it pushes against the American continent and is deflected northward by the Yucatán Peninsula. There is only one outlet for this moving mass of water and that is through the Straits of Florida, between Florida and Cuba. Soon after rounding the tip of Florida the Gulf Stream is joined by other currents from off Puerto Rico and the Bahamas.

The warm Gulf current continues northward, paralleling the eastern coast of the United States to a point off the Grand Banks, Newfoundland. Here it is met by the Labrador Current, and the two continue east as the North Atlantic Current to Europe.

The completed Ben Franklin *research submersible being made ready for a test dive. (Grumman Engineering Corporation)*

A deep blue color distinguishes the Gulf Stream from the colder, neighboring ocean waters. As the Stream passes Florida, it has a temperature of about 80° F. Its speed at this point is 3 to 4 miles per hour. This decreases with depth. The exact boundaries of the Gulf Stream are hard to fix because it has countless offshoots and changes continuously. However, it can be considered to have an average width of 50 miles.

Jacques Piccard proposed to ride the current of the Gulf Stream aboard the submerged *Ben Franklin* without using the vehicle's propulsion units. His plan was to start the "Gulf Stream Drift Mission" at a point near Miami, Florida, and end it off the coast of Halifax, Nova Scotia—a distance of more than 1,500 nautical miles. Remaining submerged within the Stream at depths ranging from 500 feet to almost 2,000 feet, the PX-15 would drift with the current's speed of about 5 miles per hour. The distance to be covered each day was estimated at between 36 and 48 nautical miles. The entire underwater trip was expected to take nearly six weeks. During this period scientists

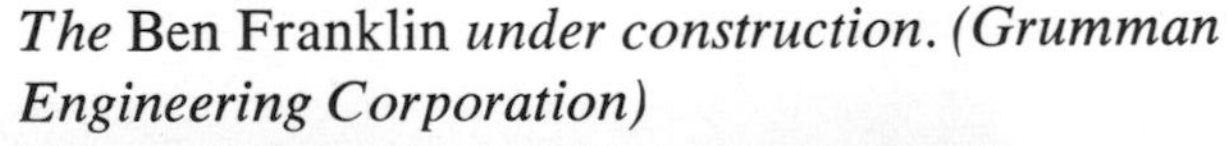

The Ben Franklin *under construction. (Grumman Engineering Corporation)*

aboard the vehicle would study the marine life, chemistry, and physical nature of the undersea portions of the Stream.

Piccard's underwater expedition was to be carried out in the most advanced type of submersible available, the PX-15. Its construction was sponsored and supervised by the Grumman Engineering Corporation of New York. The *Ben Franklin,* however, was actually built in Switzerland.

The hull of the PX-15 is made of 1⅜-inch-thick steel plate capable of withstanding 80,000 pounds of pressure per square inch. It has a length of 48 feet and a beam of 13 feet. The undersea vehicle weighs 130 tons. Hull strength is such that the PX-15 can travel underwater at a maximum depth of 2,000 feet and descend to an absolute limit of 4,000 feet before sea pressure would become dangerous.

Propulsion is provided by four 25-horsepower electric motors, two forward on either side of the hull and two at the stern end, also on either side. Each motor and attached propeller is housed in a cylindrical unit. The motors are powered by batteries arranged in banks within a compartment in the lower keel section of the hull. This compartment is open to the sea, but the lead-acid batteries themselves are encased in oil to protect them from the water.

It was not Piccard's intention to use the motors of the PX-15 in the Gulf Stream drift, except to maintain the vehicle in a desired position. The motors can be rotated from a normal forward position to point backward, up, or down. When the motor-propeller units are pointed in a vertical direction they help move the submersible up or down. If the thrust of the motors on one side of the PX-15 is made opposite to that of the motors on the other side, the vehicle can be made to turn around within its own length. On submerged travels all four motors can propel the PX-15 at a speed of almost 5 miles per hour.

Two main ballast tanks are attached to either side of the hull. These are completely flooded with seawater during underwater operations. Compressed air is used to blow the water out of the tanks when the submersible is on the surface. Buoyancy control of the PX-15 is managed by two pressure-resistant tanks located beneath the hull in the lower keel section. By controlling the amount of water entering these tanks, the vehicle can be held in a neutrally buoyant position at any depth within its operational range. Five tons of iron shot-ballast are also carried in the upper section of the hull. This can be dropped quickly when there is an emergency need to make the PX-15 rise to the surface.

The life-support system has been designed to sustain a crew of six for six weeks, with a reserve supply for two additional weeks. This system consists mainly of tanks of liquid oxygen and panels of lithium hydroxide. The latter removes dangerous carbon dioxide from the interior of the submersible. Contaminants produced by the crew's body processes, as well as by the equipment and materials within the hull, are removed by blocks of activated charcoal and by a unit employing chemical burner processes. The burner goes on automatically if the contaminants reach a dangerous level. This is measured by strategically placed sensing devices throughout the interior of the PX-15.

The interior of the research submersible has

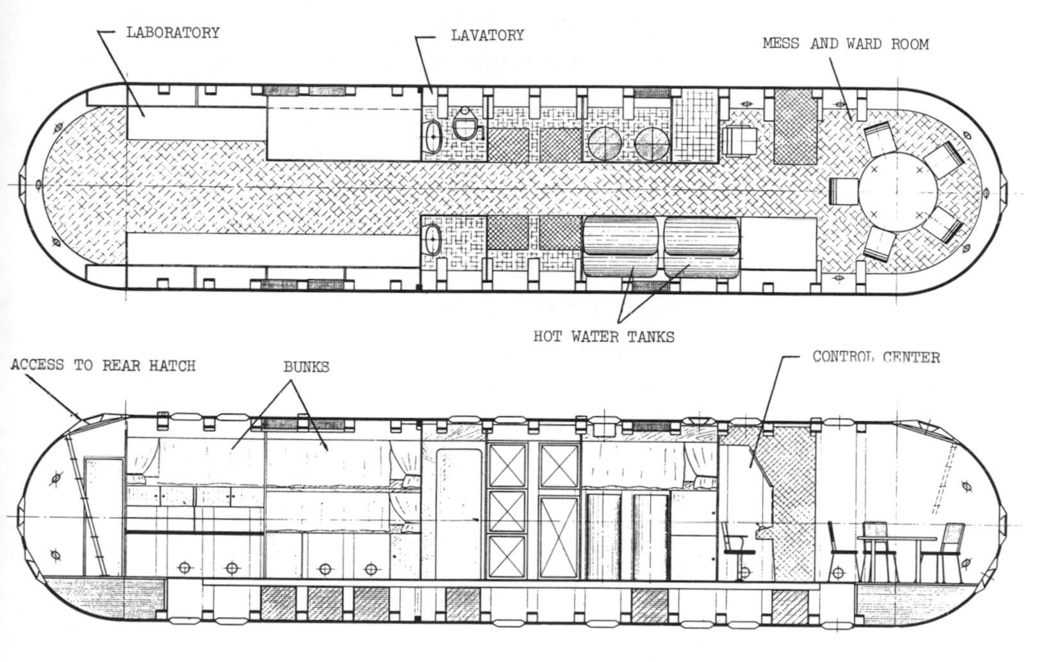

The main features of the Ben Franklin*'s interior. (Grumman Engineering Corporation)*

been compactly designed for the crew's living quarters, scientific work, and navigation. A dining and relaxation cabin is in the bow, adjoined by a navigation control room, then hot water tanks, kitchen, toilet, and shower facilities amidships; there are also bunks for the crew and, finally, in the stern, a cabin where the scientific activities of the vessel are carried out.

Two hatches fore and aft provide entrance into the submersible's interior. For viewing the underwater surroundings, the hull is pierced by twenty-nine portholes. These permit visibility in all directions. To help in viewing the undersea environment, the PX-15 carries high-powered lights along its sides, fore and aft, and underneath the hull.

An unusual installation aboard the PX-15 is super-insulated tanks filled with hot water. Maintained at a temperature of 210° F., the water is used for cooking and for bathing. The crew's food is dehydrated and prepared in such a way that it cooks quickly when placed in the scalding water. It may also be prepared with cold water if necessary. Other tanks carry drinking water.

In addition to sonar and television navigational equipment, the PX-15 also has an advanced underwater telephone apparatus that permits it to remain in constant contact with a surface support ship.

A special communications system was devised for use by the crew in the course of the Gulf Stream Drift Mission. It consists of brightly colored aluminum balls, five inches in diameter. The balls may be filled with exposed film, tape recordings, written comments, or specimens of marine life. Then the spheres are released through a special hatch in the hull and float to the surface. As they bob about on the surface of the water, the bright colors make it easy for them to be spotted by colleagues aboard a support ship or observation plane.

Throughout the Gulf Stream drift expedition the *Ben Franklin* was accompanied by a naval surface support ship. One of its chief duties was to provide Piccard and his colleagues with the exact latitude and longitude of their position as they traveled slowly northward. This information was vital to the research being carried on below. To perform this critical assignment, the support ship was outfitted with highly sophisticated equipment, including sensitive sonic detection gear.

Closely following the original Gulf Stream Drift

The Star I *on sea trials off Connecticut.*
(Allis-Chalmers Manufacturing Co.)

Mission plan, Dr. Piccard and five colleagues began their historic underwater voyage on July 14, 1969. They were towed 19 miles out to sea off Palm Beach, Florida, to catch the Gulf Stream. The oceanographers drifted northward for thirty days, covering a distance of 1,650 miles. They brought the *Ben Franklin* to the surface 400 miles south-southeast of Nova Scotia on August 14. Because the deeper portions of the Gulf Stream move much faster than estimated, the *Ben Franklin* completed the journey almost two weeks ahead of schedule.

Dr. Piccard and his fellow crew members were impressed by their smooth, serene undersea ride. This was in sharp contrast to that experienced by those aboard the surface support ship, which was knocked about by high winds and rough seas.

The research submersibles discussed thus far are by no means the only ones in existence. There are a large number of them, both in the United States and nations abroad.

Launched in 1963, the American-made *Star I* was strictly an experimental undersea vehicle built to test systems for navigation, control, communications, and life support, and to determine the reliability of new buoyancy materials. A tiny underwater craft with room for a single crewman, *Star I* measured 10 feet long and weighed 1 ton. Twin motors mounted on the sides of the hull permitted the vehicle to maneuver in all directions as well as to hover in one spot. It could travel at a speed of 1 knot at a maximum depth of 200 feet. The submersible was also able to remain submerged for four hours. *Star I* was the first underwater vehicle to run on a fuel cell, a newly developed space-age power source. This cell converts certain chemicals like hydrazine, when combined with oxygen, directly into electricity.

Star II is a more advanced, big brother to its predecessor. With a length of 17 feet and a weight of almost 5 tons, this submersible can dive to a maximum depth of 1,200 feet and remain below for as long as eight hours. Two reversible motor-propellers mounted on the vehicle's horizontal tail surface give it a speed of 4½ knots. A third motor is placed behind the entrance hatch for vertical maneuvering.

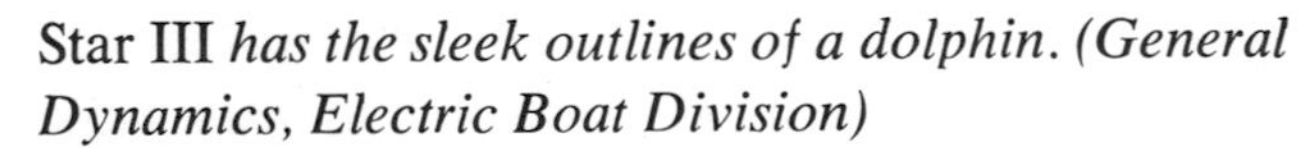

Star III *has the sleek outlines of a dolphin. (General Dynamics, Electric Boat Division)*

The research submersible Asherah *has been used mainly for underwater archaeological exploration. (General Dynamics, Electric Boat Division)*

An even larger submersible of its class, *Star III* can dive as deep as 2,000 feet, stay below for twelve hours and travel at a speed of 5 knots. It is 24½ feet long and weighs 10 tons. Its main propulsion unit is a stern-mounted motor. The vehicle also has thruster units—devices that operate like jet nozzles—for horizontal and vertical maneuvers and for hovering.

Asherah was designed and built by General Dynamics Corporation for the University of Pennsylvania. That company is also the creator of the *Star* family of undersea vehicles and builders of United States Navy nuclear submarines.

Named for the Phoenician goddess of the sea, the submersible *Asherah* is 17 feet long, weighs 4 tons, and can operate at a depth of 600 feet for ten hours. Two motors mounted on either side of the hull can propel the vehicle at a top speed of 4 knots. Used primarily to perform underwater archaeological research, *Asherah* is equipped with special cameras for three-dimensional viewing and numerous other tools.

Outstanding among its research projects was the filming of the wreck of a 1,500-year-old Byzantine galley in the Aegean Sea. The task took *Asherah* one hour. Without the help of the underwater vehicle the same filming job would have taken scuba divers several months. The *Asherah* has also been used for geological studies for the Smithsonian Institution and marine biology work for the Bureau of Commercial Fisheries and the universities of Hawaii and Rhode Island.

Deepstar 2,000 and *Deepstar 4,000* are submersibles for deep-sea research built by the Westinghouse Electric Corporation. Their names indicate the maximum depths at which they can operate. *Deepstar 2,000* is 14 feet long and weighs 4 tons. It is powered mainly by a single propeller-equipped motor. Two water jets are also used in maneuvering the vehicle. The submersible's life-support system can maintain a two-man crew for forty-eight hours. It has two mechanical arms.

Deepstar 4,000 is 4 feet longer than *Deepstar 2,000* and capable of diving twice as deep. Two

A diver engaged in underwater archaeological research. This is a seventh-century shipwreck excavated by the University of Pennsylvania Museum. (University of Pennsylvania Museum, National Geographic Society Expedition)

Deepstar 4,000 *prowling over the ocean floor.*
(Westinghouse Underseas Division)

motors can propel it at a top speed of 3 knots. It weighs close to 10 tons. The underwater vehicle's design and control is such that it can climb at a 60-degree angle and dive at a 50-degree angle.

Japan made its debut in the design and construction of underwater research vehicles with the *Kuroshio I*. The work of professors at Hokkaido University, the vehicle was more a diving chamber than a submarine in appearance. It was not free to move around underwater but was connected by a steel cable to a surface support ship. Motors were added to the vehicle later, permitting it some limited undersea movement.

The *Kuroshio I* made its first descent in 1951 and was used for six years thereafter for underwater research by Japanese scientists. The vehicle made almost 400 dives at an average depth of 600 feet.

A redesigned and improved *Kuroshio II* was built in 1960. More like a submarine than its earlier model, this undersea vehicle has a length of 38 feet and weighs close to 12 tons. Although equipped with a motor and propeller the research submersible is still connected to a surface support ship by means of a cable. This cable supplies its electric power and telephone communications. The *Kuroshio II* can carry six crew members. Its life-support system can sustain the crew for up to twenty-four hours at a maximum depth of 650 feet. Like its predecessor, the *Kuroshio II* is used mainly for marine biological research.

The *Yomiuri,* another Japanese undersea research vehicle, is more advanced than the two just

This Japanese research submersible, the Yomiuri*, can travel with equal ease above or below the sea.*
(The Yomiuri Shimbun, Japan)

The Yomiuri *surrounded by curious fish. (The Yomiuri Shimbun, Japan)*

described. Completed in 1964, this submersible has a length of 48 feet, a beam of 8 feet, and weighs more than 30 tons. It can be driven underwater by one electric and two diesel motors at a speed of 4 knots. The *Yomiuri* carries a crew of six and is capable of operating at a depth of 1,000 feet.

The *Yomiuri* was built to make studies in marine biology; measure various aspects of the ocean environment—currents, salinity, temperature; and explore the geological nature of the sea floor. These researches have two main goals. The first is simply a desire for more knowledge about the ocean environment. The second is to understand better the biology of finfish and shellfish for increased food production.

The *Severyanka* is a Russian undersea research craft. Redesigned from a conventional naval submarine, the *Severyanka* was developed for oceanographic studies and for fisheries research. It is

240 feet long, has a beam of 22 feet, and weighs more than 1,100 tons. The huge undersea vehicle requires a crew of sixty, including scientific personnel. Completed in 1958, it is driven by a powerful diesel-electric propulsion system that gives it a cruising speed of 15 knots. The *Severyanka* is capable of diving to 550 feet. It can travel over long distances, for as much as 16,500 miles. A snorkel ventilation system enables the underwater craft to stay submerged for long periods.

SURV (Standard Underwater Research Vehicle) is the first vehicle of its kind to be constructed in England. A small submersible, it measures 10 feet long and 6 feet wide and weighs 6 tons. A two-man crew operates the vehicle. SURV's life-support equipment has an operating period of thirty-six hours. Two electrically driven propellers power the miniature underwater craft. The propellers can be pointed at different angles. Thus SURV can move in almost any direction desired. It has a speed of 2.5 knots, a range of close to 70 miles, and can dive to 600 feet.

Ten viewing ports are set into the crew's pressureproof compartment. The crew is further aided by mechanical arms, sea-bottom drills, and still and motion picture cameras.

SURV was created primarily for studies in marine biology and for performing geological analyses of the seabed. But it is versatile enough to also be used for everyday undersea jobs such as the inspection of telephone cables and oil and natural gas pipelines. In addition SURV can conduct emergency search and recovery operations.

These research submersibles are among the first of their kind, as much pioneers as the man-made vehicles now spinning through the world of outer space. Today's oceanographers have tools unlike any previously available for advancing the study of the world's oceans. As man gains experience in the deep-ocean world, even more versatile and more efficient underwater vehicles are being planned and built.

An artist's drawing of a completed undersea oil-wellhead installation. The scuba divers are about to board their work submersible, Beaver Mark IV, *for the return trip to the surface. (Ocean Systems Operations, North American Rockwell Corporation)*

Chapter 3
Work submersibles

Deep-diving submersibles can perform many valuable underwater tasks of economic importance. Submersibles are considered ideal for the inspection and repair of underwater telephone cables and oil and gas pipelines; for salvage work; and for surveys of the ocean bottom. Future roles foreseen for these vehicles are drilling for oil, mining offshore mineral-ore deposits, and conducting radically new fishing operations.

Oceanographers interested in the development and uses of submersibles feel that they are the key by which man will unlock the riches of the oceans.

A number of the early submersibles, such as *Star III,* carried on both scientific activities and engineering or work projects. From the experience gained with these vehicles, designers of submersibles are gradually developing a true undersea work boat. One of the pioneer models is the *Beaver Mark IV,* built by the Ocean Systems Operations division of the North American Rockwell Corporation.

Beaver Mark IV is a short, stubby work boat that was first launched in 1968. It is 24 feet long, with a beam of 9½ feet, and 8½ feet high—small enough to be easily transported by cargo plane to any ocean area for a work assignment. The weight of the submersible is close to 27,000 pounds, and it has a diving range of 2,000 feet.

The *Beaver Mark IV* consists of two spherical chambers of high-strength steel, enclosed by an outer, streamlined shell. The sealed spherical chambers, called the pressure hull, are designed to withstand water pressure at 2,000 feet. They are located fore and aft and connected by a narrow tunnel. Both pressure chambers have room for two crew members. A pilot and observer oc-

Diagrams of the main features of the Beaver Mark IV *work submersible. (Ocean Systems Operations, North American Rockwell Corporation)*

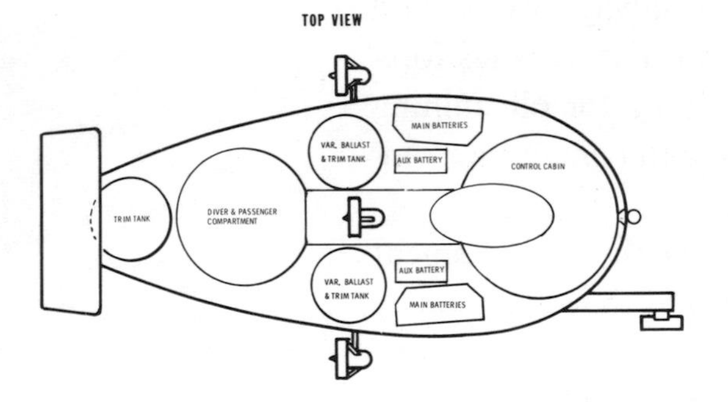

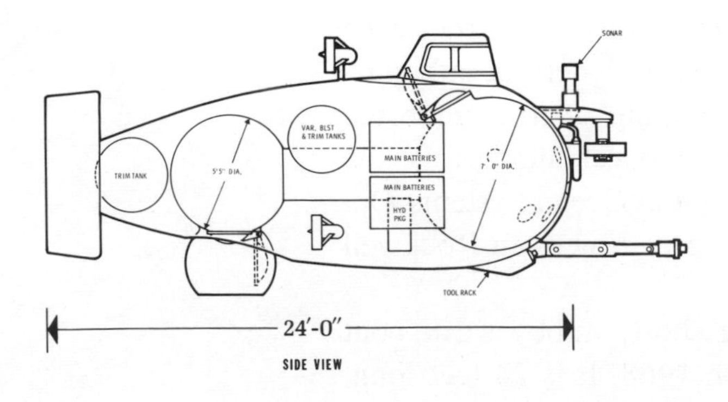

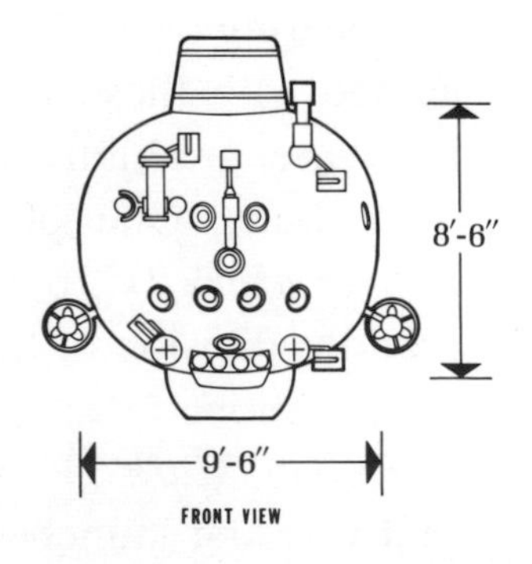

cupy the forward chamber; the rear chamber is normally used by two divers.

The aft pressure chamber has a funnel-shaped extension or skirt that protrudes downward through the outer shell. Various devices called adapters can be bolted to this skirt so that the work sub may be joined to another submarine or an underwater structure. Inside the skirt is a hatch leading into the rear pressure chamber. Divers can enter or exit the *Beaver Mark IV* through this hatch while the vehicle is submerged. This is possible when a specific amount of air pressure is maintained inside the chamber.

If the air pressure inside the chamber is made to match the water pressure outside the submersible, the hatch cover may be opened without fear of water entering. This enables divers to come and go as they wish. Should the submersible operate at a 200-foot depth, the water pressure amounts to about 88.2 pounds per square inch. This is six times the air pressure (14.7 pounds) at sea level.

Before the hatch of the *Beaver Mark IV* can be safely opened at the 200-foot depth, the air pressure inside the rear chamber must be built up to equal the outside water pressure. Cylinders of compressed air carried in the submersible are used for this purpose.

After divers have completed their mission in the sea, and returned to the sphere, the hatch cover is securely locked and the air pressure slowly reduced to that existing at sea level. This procedure is called decompression. It may also take place in a special decompression tank aboard a surface support ship or on shore. In this case the work submersible is hoisted out of the water and its mating skirt attached to that on the decompression tank.

A full-scale mock-up of the Beaver Mark IV. *(Ocean Systems Operations, North American Rockwell Corporation)*

The outer, streamlined hull of the *Beaver Mark IV* is made of aluminum and several removable fiberglass panels. The latter provide easy access to vital equipment for repairs or adjustments. When the submersible is beneath the sea the outer hull becomes flooded. Enclosed by this open outer hull are the vehicle's two main ballast tanks. These, along with a variable ballast and trim system, provide the crew of the *Beaver* with a means for precisely controlling its movements underwater. Ballast and trim systems also allow for necessary corrections when changes take place in the vehicle's buoyancy as it descends and ascends. The *Beaver* has been designed to be light enough to carry a 2,000-pound payload of tools or equipment for an underwater project.

Beaver's propulsion system consists of three propeller-equipped electric motors arranged on either side of the hull and on top. The power for these motors is obtained from a main lead-acid battery source.

At the tail is a large, ring-shaped shroud, within

which are crossed horizontal and vertical fins. Movable sections on the vertical fin help in turning to the right or left; similar sections on the horizontal fin aid the submersible in making up and down maneuvers.

When traveling underwater the *Beaver* can move at a cruise speed of 2½ knots for a period of twelve hours. If sudden bursts of high speed are required, it is capable of reaching 5 knots and holding this for twenty minutes.

Each of the *Beaver*'s spherical hulls has a life-support system with a duration of forty-eight hours. This consists of a self-contained oxygen supply and a unit holding lithium hydroxide to remove carbon dioxide.

The *Beaver*'s forward section has ten viewing ports that provide the crew with a good view of the work area. The nose section is fitted with an extendable boom that carries a light to further illuminate the work scene. Also on the front of the work boat are a movable television camera and a still camera.

Two highly dexterous mechanical arms, or manipulators, are attached to the submersible's front end. They can hold and exchange from one arm to the other such tools as wire brushes, wrenches, a stud gun (electrical power wrench), an explosive hammer, a cable-cutter, and a claw grip. The *Beaver* was created to build undersea oil rigs, salvage sunken vessels, and inspect dock pilings and the submerged portions of sea walls.

Edwin A. Link, one of America's foremost pioneers in underwater activities, has designed in cooperation with Perry Submarine Builders an underwater work boat called the *Deep Diver*. Built in Florida and tested in the offshore waters of that state, the *Deep Diver* has been described as the

The Deep Diver *submersible in the process of being launched. (Ocean Systems, Inc.)*

first truly operational work submersible. Not only capable of transporting divers, tools, and equipment to and from an undersea work site, *Deep Diver* can also remain at the underwater location to serve as a rest shelter for the sea-bottom workers.

Deep Diver, like the *Beaver* and other submersibles of the same type, has two separate pressure chambers of half-inch-thick steel. These crew chambers are connected by a hatch. A streamlined fiberglass shell covers the chambers, giving the underwater work boat an overall length of 22 feet and a beam of 5 feet. The vehicle weighs slightly more than 8 tons.

The life-support system of the *Deep Diver* can supply its four-man crew (two in each pressure chamber) with breathable air for up to twenty-four hours. The air is kept at 14.7 pounds of pressure per square inch. This allows crew members to travel in a comfortable, shirt-sleeve environment no matter how deep the submersible descends. The atmosphere breathed is a mixture of helium, nitrogen, and oxygen. These gases are stored in steel cylinders outside the pressure chambers. Divers working outside the submersible also tap this gas mixture by means of an air hose.

The *Deep Diver*'s rear pressure chamber is for the use of divers. The chamber has a hatch in the floor that can be opened when the air pressure inside is equal to the water pressure outside the submersible. Divers exit and reenter the chamber through this hatch.

Deep Diver has a main hatch and conning tower on its forward end. Eight portholes circle the wall of the conning tower, providing the pilot with a full 360 degrees of visibility. The work submersible also has thirteen additional viewing ports piercing its hull.

The *Deep Diver* is extremely maneuverable. It can go forward, backward, up, down, sideways, and even turn completely around like a spinning top. The work vehicle's fishlike movements are achieved by means of a main propeller, battery powered, which is fixed to the stern. This driving unit can be swiveled 90 degrees to the left or right. Also, on the top and bottom of the stern end, are

This diver has just emerged from the Deep Diver *through a lockout chamber in the rear. The diver may reenter the submersible in the same way. (Ocean Systems, Inc.)*

movable thrusters. These release jets of pressurized water that drive the submersible up or down, depending on the position of the thrusters.

Another propeller is attached to the nose of the submersible, but it points sideward rather than straight ahead. Covered by a cone-shaped shroud, this propeller can be rotated a complete 360 degrees. When operating, it can turn the bow of the submersible in any direction.

Deep Diver's normal operating depth is 1,250 feet. While underwater it can move at a top speed of 3 knots. When diving or rising to the surface, it moves at a rate of 2 feet per second. Power for *Deep Diver*'s surface and underwater journeys is provided by a bank of twenty lead-acid storage batteries.

This Link-Perry submersible was created to be an everyday work vehicle with almost the entire

On the right, the manipulator arm of a submersible is testing a new U-shaped tool designed to turn the valve on this typical underwater oil installation. (Ocean Systems Operations, North American Rockwell Corporation)

continental shelf within range of its diving ability. Some undersea tasks for which *Deep Diver* is especially suited are the building and maintenance of well heads in offshore oil installations and the laying and repair of undersea oil and gas pipelines. *Deep Diver* can also lay, inspect, and maintain underwater communications cables. For salvage operations this small work submersible could serve not only as an excellent base for scuba divers to work from, but also as a transport for carrying salvaged items to the surface.

One role for which the designers of *Deep Diver* feel their vehicle has particular value is the performance of rescue missions within its diving range. Divers—especially those wearing conventional hard-hat gear—working on an installation where their air-hose lines might become entangled with undersea obstructions could summon help and receive it quickly from a rescue team traveling aboard the *Deep Diver*.

The DOWB (Deep Ocean Work Boat) is another in the growing family of work submersibles. Slightly smaller than the other work vehicles discussed, DOWB has an overall length of 17 feet and a beam of 8½ feet. It is constructed in much the same way as the others except that it has only a single spherical, inner pressure chamber. The spherical compartment is formed of extremely strong steel to allow the vehicle to dive to depths of more than 6,000 feet. It was designed by engineers of the AC Electronics-Defense Research Laboratories of the General Motors Corporation.

The pressure chamber of the DOWB has room for a two-man crew. They can remain submerged for a period of up to sixty-five hours.

Four electrically driven motors power the work

boat both on the surface and underwater. Two motors are positioned on top of the hull for moving the vehicle in a vertical direction, and two are placed on each side of the body near the stern for horizontal travel. Normal speed of the DOWB is 2 knots, which can be maintained for two hours.

DOWB crewmen have 360 degrees of visibility with the help of a periscope-type viewing apparatus. This permits them to see the underwater region above and below their vehicle. Fathometers attached to the bottom and top sections of the hull measure the distance between DOWB and the surface of the sea as well as between the vehicle and the ocean floor. A highly sensitive sonar unit tells the pilot of any obstacles in front of the vehicle. This can also locate objects related to the submersible's work assignment.

A particularly valuable safety device among the DOWB's equipment is a sonic beacon. By con-

The streamlined outer shell of DOWB is made of fiberglass. Here it is being lowered over the steel pressure sphere that serves as the two-man crew compartment. (AC Electronics, General Motors Corporation)

The mechanical arm of the DOWB work submersible being tested on the ocean floor. (AC Electronics, General Motors Corporation)

stantly emitting sound waves, the sonic beacon helps those aboard a surface support ship to know at all times the position of the undersea work boat. Additional communication with a mother ship is available through an underwater radiotelephone.

Attached to the manipulator arm of the work submersible is a television viewing system. While the arm is operated from within the cabin, the television camera allows the operator to move it with great precision for complex or heavy lifting chores. The manipulator, vital for DOWB's ability to perform work, has a reach of 49 inches and can lift objects weighing up to 50 pounds.

When the work in which DOWB is involved requires the vehicle to be positioned firmly on the sea floor, it rests on two skids attached on either side of the bottom of the hull. These are similar to the skids on some small helicopters that are used instead of wheels for landing.

The *Pisces* is an aptly named underwater work boat. Its name refers to the zodiacal constellation that is in the form of a fish. The man-made *Pisces* is a small, rugged work vehicle with a length of 16 feet—slightly longer than an automobile—and a beam of 11½ feet. Like most of the current family of work and research submersibles, the heart of *Pisces'* construction consists of two spheres formed of high-strength steel. The spherical pressure chambers are enclosed in a streamlined shell and permit the vehicle to dive to a depth of 5,000 feet.

This underwater work boat is powered by two electrically driven propellers mounted on either side of the hull. The *Pisces* has a cruising speed of 1 knot and a top speed of 6 knots. It can cruise for twenty-four hours or travel at the top rate for seven hours. A low speed is more important for work and research submersibles than high speed because this permits better observation of the sea environment.

The *Pisces* can stay submerged for a normal period of twenty-four hours. If necessary, an auxiliary life-support unit can extend this period to seventy-two hours. For navigation and work activities, the *Pisces* is equipped with a sonar system that scans the sea in an arc of 180 degrees. The vehicle has two manipulators and a powerful clamping arm. The arm holds the work boat on the sea bottom if the nature of the work requires this.

The *Pisces* was designed and built for seabed oil-drilling work, for maintenance of underwater oil rigs and telephone cables, and for underwater mining activities.

One of the deepest-diving members of the family of work submersibles is *Deep Quest*. Designed and built by Lockheed Missiles & Space Company, this undersea vehicle has the outward look of a miniature conventional submarine. Showing the influence of aviation in its creation, the craft has a vertical rudder at the stern along with small, horizontal, plane surfaces. Many airplanes have a similar tail structure. *Deep Quest* has a length of 39 feet, a beam of 19 feet, and weighs 54 tons. The vehicle's pressure compartment consists of two intersecting spheres made of high-strength steel, large enough to accommodate two crewmen and two observers.

The propulsion system of the *Deep Quest* consists of two electric motors for the main driving force and two electrically powered thrusters to assist the vehicle's up and down maneuvers.

Capable of operating to depths of 8,000 feet, the *Deep Quest* can attain a speed of 4½ knots. At a slower rate the vehicle may travel submerged for as long as twenty-four hours. The craft's life-support system can sustain its four-man crew for the same period. There is a safety unit permitting the system to operate for an additional forty-eight hours in an emergency.

Deep Quest *is capable of operating at depths of more than 6,000 feet. On one test dive it reached a depth of 8,310 feet—a record for submarines of its type. (Lockheed Missiles and Space Co.)*

The *Deep Quest,* a powerful underwater work boat, can transport a 3,400-pound cargo of tools, supplies, and equipment. It was created primarily to carry out underwater explorations at extreme depths. It can make surveys for mineral deposits and help in underwater engineering activities such as the laying and repair of undersea communications cables and the construction of oil-drilling rigs on the sea bottom.

Another new deep-diving underwater work boat is almost a twin of the Grumman-Piccard PX-15. Still in the design stage, this undersea vehicle is identified as GSV-1, Grumman Submersible Vehicle #1.

The GSV-1 will be larger than the PX-15, with a length of 61 feet, a beam of 19 feet, and a weight of 173 tons. It will be capable of operating at the same depths as the PX-15—to 2,000 feet. Propulsion will be by means of three electrically powered motors. Two will be located on either side of the hull. They will be capable of turning in a horizontal or vertical position. A third motor and propeller are to be installed on the lower part of the stern. They will help in maneuvering the underwater work boat. The GSV-1's power units will give it a maximum submerged speed of about 4 knots.

For its underwater work activities, the GSV-1 will carry a crew of nine men. Three will be stationed in the forward pressure chamber and six will perform their duties in the aft chamber. A hatch 4 feet in diameter will connect the two compartments so that the crew may move easily between them. The submersible's life-support system will permit the crew to stay submerged for two weeks. In the course of its work operations, the

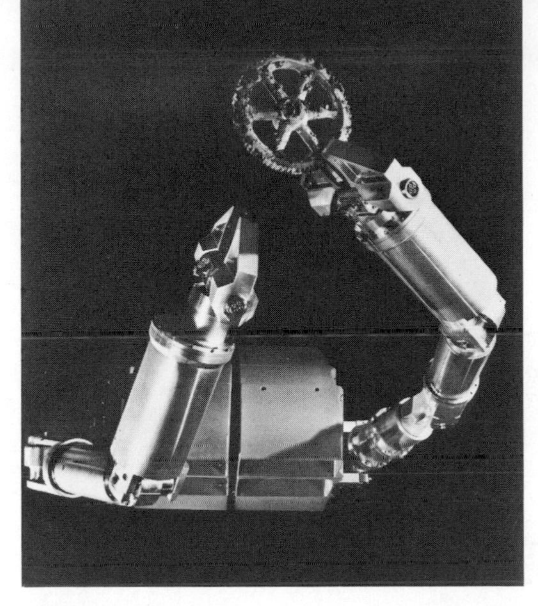

This is one of many types of mechanical manipulators —robot arms and hands—used on work submersibles to pick up objects from the floor of the sea. (General Dynamics, Electric Boat Division)

GSV-1 is expected to handle easily loads of supplies and equipment weighing up to 9 tons.

One feature that makes the GSV-1 differ in appearance from the PX-15 is a pontoon landing-gear structure attached to the bottom portion of the hull. It is to serve as a firm base when the submarine rests on the bottom of the sea. Steadying the vehicle in this manner will enable the manipulator to be used more effectively. The landing gear is also expected to be a convenient mounting place for containers carrying tools and equipment or holding objects to be brought up from the sea bottom.

Still another feature that will make the GSV-1 different from its predecessor is a lockout compartment. This is a separate spherical unit 8 feet in diameter. It is bolted to the rear pressure chamber, and a hatch provides entry from one unit to another. Divers may plunge into the sea through

The Swimmer Sled being put through its paces undersea. (Ocean Systems Operations, North American Rockwell Corporation)

another and larger hatch in the bottom of this lockout compartment.

The life-support system aboard the GSV-1 will employ a mixture of helium and oxygen. The system is designed to operate efficiently even though the submersible is cruising 1,500 feet beneath the sea. At this underwater level, where the pressure is more than forty-five atmospheres, the interior pressure of the GSV-1 will be maintained at one atmosphere.

This advanced underwater submersible will have a manipulator with a reach of 10 feet and the ability to lift 500 pounds. Sensitive sonar devices will assist in navigating the vehicle. In addition to radiotelephone equipment for communicating with a surface support ship, the GSV-1 will have an intercommunications system between the crew compartments.

Two small, unusual underwater vehicles have been created by the builders of the *Beaver Mark*

IV work submersible. The first of these is an open-deck, miniature submarine of great maneuverability. The Swimmer Sled, as it is called, can carry two scuba divers through ocean or lake waters at depths to 150 feet and at a submerged speed of 2½ knots. Riding the vehicle as though it were a porpoise, divers can skim along on or below the water's surface, make steep dives or climbs, negotiate hairpin turns, and "stop on a dime"—all without moving more than a single control stick.

The steel Swimmer Sled is 13 feet long, weighs half a ton, and is moved by an electrically driven 8-inch propeller. Lead-acid batteries, of the kind used in automobiles, supply the power. The underwater vehicle also has a recessed instrument panel for the pilot, containing a compass and indicators showing depth, battery life, ballast, and air supply. The control stick operated by the pilot works two forward horizontal fins as well as the aft rudder for steering the vehicle.

Both the pilot and his companion lie facedown on the miniature underwater ferry, one in front of the other. There are fixed handholds and footholds for the diver riding in the rear position. Underarm shoulder supports, resembling those on the tops of crutches, are attached at the front end.

The Swimmer Sled was created to transport scuba divers to and from undersea work sites. But it is also used by divers inspecting the submerged sections of sea walls, docks, hulls of vessels, pipelines, and telephone cables. It may be employed, too, for underwater research and rescue missions and for carrying camera equipment to make undersea motion picture or television scenes.

In open-sea tests off Catalina Island, California,

This miniature submarine Swimmer Sled is designed to carry divers between surface ships and underwater work installations. (Ocean Systems Operations, North American Rockwell Corporation)

the Swimmer Sled demonstrated its agility by diving down at angles of 60 degrees to the surface and soaring up to the surface in a nearly vertical position.

Engineers who created the Swimmer Sled have proposed a larger model that could carry twice as many divers. This miniature submarine ferry would be constructed largely of fiberglass and would measure 15 feet in length and 4 feet in diameter. Driven by an electrically powered propeller, it would have a top speed of 5 knots. Vertical and horizontal fins at the stern end would provide the main means for maneuvering the submerged ferry up, down, right, or left. Its maximum diving range would be close to 400 feet.

Divers riding this advanced underwater ferry would travel in an open, water-filled cabin. They would wear scuba equipment. However, the flooded cabin would eliminate the need for a complex pressurized air system as well as for a bulky air lock. In order that the scuba divers might conserve their own individual air supplies, a tank of oxygen—into which they could plug their air lines while riding—would be carried on the vehicle.

For steering the underwater ferry a pilot would use a hand-operated stick mechanically linked to the vertical and horizontal fins at the stern.

The design of rescue vessels is increasingly occupying the talents of engineers building underwater vehicles. The need for rescue submersibles was made painfully clear when the nuclear submarines *Thresher* and *Scorpion* met disaster. There was no equipment in existence that could have been used to aid the crewmen if there had been a possibility that they were still alive aboard the wrecked undersea craft.

The DSRV-1 (Deep Submergence Rescue Vehicle-1) is the first American attempt to build a submersible strictly for undersea search and rescue

A diagram of the procedure to be followed when the Navy's Deep Submergence Rescue Vehicle (DSRV) is sent on an emergency rescue mission. (U.S. Navy)

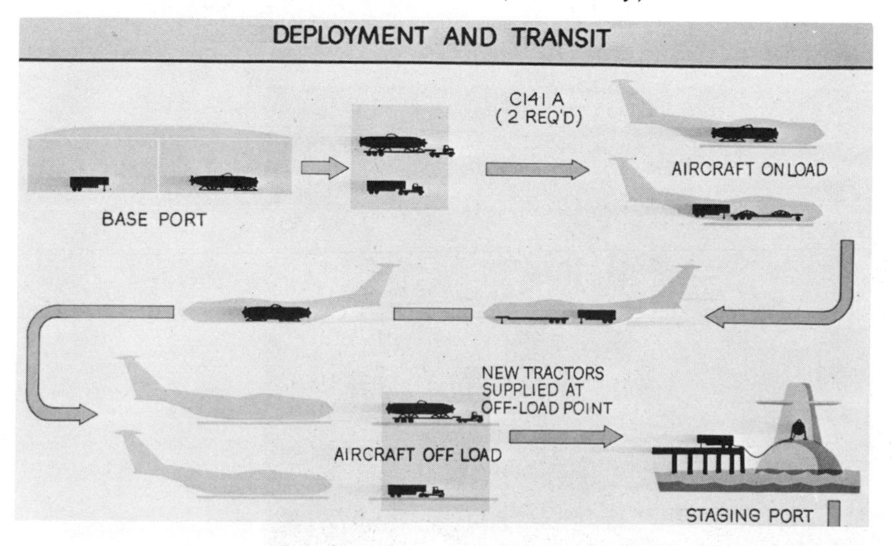

work. The United States Navy is supporting the development of this vehicle. In outward appearance the DSRV-1 looks much like any other submarine. It is a small vessel whose overall size, 49 feet in length and 8 feet in diameter, has been determined by the carrying capacity of giant cargo planes. The rescue submersible is designed to be transported by air so that it can reach the scene of a disaster in the shortest possible time.

The DSRV-1 will then ride "piggyback" aboard a nuclear submarine to the emergency site. Although capable of diving to 5,000 feet, the rescue submersible itself has a comparatively limited range and speed for underwater travel. It would take too long under its own power to reach a submarine stricken several hundred miles from the nearest land base.

Though it may not be able to travel far, the DSRV-1 has great maneuverability—an important asset for its rescue work. This is accomplished by means of a main propeller drive unit attached to

This drawing shows how the DSRV will attach itself to a mother submarine for a "piggyback" ride. (U.S. Navy)

the stern and four thruster devices placed at the forward and aft ends of the vessel.

Precise navigation and steering actions will be required while the DSRV-1 is involved in a rescue mission. To help the pilot and copilot with these tasks the submersible is equipped with a complex group of operating and navigating instruments. One of the most important is a computer. This will be fed a variety of information by the pilot and his assistant concerning such matters as depth, power output of the sub's engines, and speed of the underwater current through which they are moving. After swiftly digesting all this data, the computer will produce answers for the proper running and guidance of the submersible.

To aid rescue missions, DSRV-1 has television cameras fore, aft, and on top, as well as a manipulator. Its most important rescue feature, however, is a mating transfer hatch and skirt. This is an outside extension of the vehicle's entry hatch on the bottom of the hull. During a rescue maneuver the transfer skirt is joined to the hatch of a disabled submarine. After the two hatches are secured water is pumped out of the skirt section, permitting submariners to move from their disabled vessel to the rescue submersible above.

Developing the mating transfer hatch of the DSRV-1 and the techniques for its use were the most difficult problems faced by the vehicle's designers. After finding a disabled submarine, rescuers then have to locate the exact position of its escape hatch. At extreme ocean depths, which are in total darkness, to find any object is a near-impossible task. To enable rescuers to perform this vital part of their assignment, engineers equipped the DSRV-1 with the most advanced underwater optical and sonic sensors. These uncanny devices

An illustration of how the DSRV will rescue survivors from a damaged submarine. The DSRV will be able to pick up twenty-four men at a time. (U.S. Navy)

permit the rescue submersible to "see" as well as "feel" unseen objects.

The next phase is to effectively and safely "mate" the hatches of the stranded submarine and the rescue submersible. The constant movement of the sea adds enormously to the difficulty of this step. Jet thrusters provide much of the answer to the problem. They make it possible for the rescue vehicle to hover over its "landing" area much like a helicopter about to set down on a landing pad.

The pressure compartment of the DSRV-1 is composed of three spheres, each 7½ feet in diameter. These are located amidships and are interconnected by hatches. The front chamber is used for the control and navigation of the undersea vessel. The pilot and copilot operate from this compartment. The other two chambers are for rescued personnel and a third crewman. These compartments have a capacity for twenty-four men.

Electric motors powered by storage batteries spin the DSRV-1's conventional stern propeller. This propeller, together with the four thrusters, allows the rescue vehicle to maneuver and hover in underwater currents as strong as 1 knot. The undersea rescue boat has a maximum speed of 5 knots and a cruising speed of 3 knots that it can maintain for twelve hours.

The United States Navy is developing still another deep-ocean submersible designed mainly for search and underwater-survey operations. Known as the Deep Submergence Search Vehicle (DSSV), it will be capable of traveling normally at depths of 20,000 feet, almost four miles down. The external hull will be made of lightweight corrosion-resistant materials, such as fiberglass. The internal pressure chamber, constructed of high-strength steel, will have room for two operators and two relief men.

The DSSV will be 50 feet long and will have a diameter of 11 feet. Its maximum weight will be 35 tons. This advanced submersible will be constructed in such a way that, like the DSRV-1, it will be able to ride "piggyback" on a large submarine. For its own propulsion system electric motors powered by storage batteries or fuel cells are being considered. The underwater vehicle is expected to have a maximum speed of 5 knots and a cruising speed of 3 knots. At the latter rate it will have a travel endurance of thirty hours. Control equipment and the needed life-support system are to be similar to the equipment developed for the DSRV-1.

Once it successfully completes sea trials, the DSSV will be capable of traveling over almost 98 percent of the ocean floor. Only the deepest

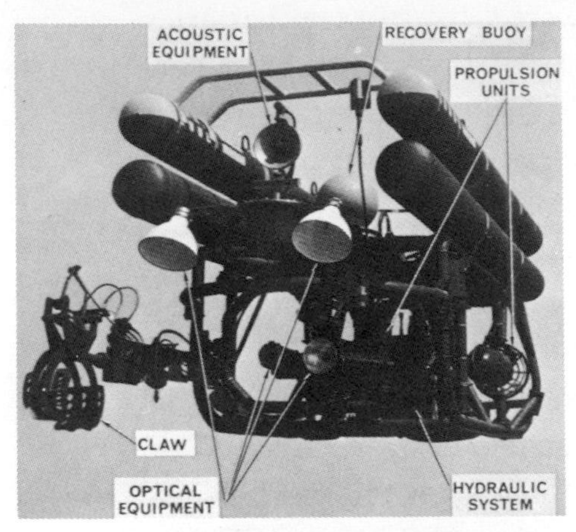

The Controlled Underwater Recovery Vehicle (CURV) is an unmanned robot built to raise objects from the ocean bottom. Its claw and propulsion motors are controlled from the surface with the help of closed-circuit television. (U.S. Navy)

trenches, such as the one in which the *Trieste* made its record-breaking dive, will be off limits for this deep-diving submersible.

When not on rescue missions, the DSSV will be employed in research projects. For this type of activity it will be equipped with a powerful manipulator and claw for recovering objects and specimens from the sea floor.

Unmanned, robot underwater vehicles are a branch of the submersibles family now being used for ocean-floor search and work missions. These unmanned submersibles are either towed close to the sea bottom or are self-propelled. Their equipment is operated electrically from a mother ship. The United States Navy has developed several models for the recovery of unexploded bombs and torpedoes on test-firing ranges at sea. Most successful of these is the Controlled Underwater Recovery Vehicle (CURV).

CURV is a tethered, unmanned submersible 5 feet high, 6 feet wide, and 13 feet long—about the same length as the average automobile. It consists of an open frame of aluminum tubing with four large buoyancy tanks mounted on its top and two on each side. Maneuvering is accomplished with three small motors—two positioned on the sides for horizontal travel and a third positioned vertically for up and down movement. These units not only provide propulsion but, by means of their weight, help keep the vehicle down on the sea floor.

Work equipment carried by the CURV includes an optical system of powerful lights, a television camera, a motion picture camera, and a strobe light. It also has a highly sensitive sonar unit for locating undersea objects. Further, the underwater robot carries a powerful, hydraulically operated steel claw for grabbing and lifting heavy objects from the ocean floor. This claw, like all of the vehicle's equipment, is monitored and operated by a team of five men at a control console aboard a mother ship.

CURV has a number of advantages over manned submersibles, including the ability to operate with unlimited endurance, day or night, at depths of 2,500 feet. It eliminates the need for human divers and is less expensive to build and operate than manned vehicles. CURV is capable of performing a number of the same undersea jobs, including surveys of the ocean floor and the inspection and maintenance of underwater pipelines and telephone cables. But CURV was originally created for raising objects from the bottom of the sea. It proved its excellence for this kind of underwater work in 1960 by bringing to the surface the

The Submerged Object Recovery Device (SORD) is another Navy-developed robot for salvaging underwater objects. It picks up sunken items with a snare. (U.S. Navy)

H-bomb that had accidentally fallen into the sea off the coast of Spain.

SORD (Submerged Object Recovery Device) is another of the undersea robots developed by the United States Navy. Designed for deep-ocean tasks, SORD picks up objects with a snare that is manipulated from a surface ship by operators who "see" what they are doing with the help of a closed-circuit television system. Cameras attached to SORD's framework function as its eyes.

A different type of unmanned underwater vehicle has been developed by scientists at the Applied Physics Laboratory of the University of Washington. It is untethered, self-propelled, and shaped like a cigar. This submersible was created for oceanographic research, including underwater acoustics. It follows a controlled undersea path. This is managed by a type of sonar guidance system operated from a surface ship. The vehicle collects such data as the velocity of sound underwater and the temperature, salinity, and other physical properties of the sea. These are recorded and stored on instruments carried aboard the submersible.

The cigar-shaped robot is 122 inches long and 20 inches in diameter. It is powered by an electric motor and a stern-mounted propeller. The vehicle weighs 1,030 pounds and can carry an additional scientific-instrument load of a little more than 100 pounds. It is capable of operating at a maximum depth of 13,000 feet and traveling at a speed of 6 knots for a period of up to five hours.

A drawing of the Navy's undersea habitat, Sealab III, and its support ship above. Electric power, communications, and other needs are provided by the support ship. The transfer capsule at the end of one of the cables transports the aquanauts to and from Sealab III. (U.S. Navy)

Chapter 4
Ocean habitats and diving chambers

Work submersibles are not the only means by which the wealth of the oceans will be exploited. Manned underwater stations—ocean habitats—promise to play an equally important role in this endeavor. Colonizing the sea floor with permanent manned stations is not a fantasy. It is as feasible as the building and occupation of manned stations in space, ideas that have already been demonstrated in an elementary way.

The idea of living and working on the bottom of the sea is not a wholly modern one. Simon Lake, who built one of the first workable submarines in the United States, wrote of the possibility of establishing an undersea supply depot for submarines over half a century ago. Lake's plan was for submariners to bring their vessels to the underwater depot, leave through an escape hatch, and enter the supply house for their needs. Their wants satisfied, the undersea travelers would return to their submarines and sail off. Another idea involving a portable manned sea-floor home was advanced by Sir Robert H. Davis in the 1920's.

These proposed ocean dwellings were never

built. The concepts were too advanced for the technology of the time. Building materials, tools, and other equipment necessary for their construction were not available until the modern age of engineering.

Now, under the experienced guidance of such outstanding oceanographers as Jacques-Yves Cousteau, Captain George F. Bond of the United States Navy, and Edwin A. Link, the first pioneer dwellings under the sea have been built.

Jacques-Yves Cousteau called his home under the sea Conshelf I—a contraction of Continental Shelf Station One. The structure was a steel chamber 17 feet long and 8 feet high. In 1962 it was lowered into the Mediterranean Sea off the coast of Marseille, France. Eight heavy chains were used to anchor the underwater house 7 feet off the bottom of the sea and 33 feet below the sea's surface.

Part of the Conshelf I experiment was to see what effects prolonged living beneath the sea would have on man. The test began on September 14, 1962, when two of Cousteau's colleagues descended to their underwater home. For seven days the aquanauts worked, ate, slept, and relaxed in the watery realm. Five hours of each day were spent outside the chamber, which the men left and entered through a hatch in the floor. Using scuba gear, they performed prearranged tasks, such as building fish pens, as they swam about.

After several hours in the sea the aquanauts found the warm, dry atmosphere inside the habitat a relief. The temperature inside the chamber was maintained in the comfortable mid-70-degree range. This was accomplished with the help of infrared heaters placed strategically throughout the interior of the sea house.

Cousteau's sea habitat was connected to the

surface by power and air lines extending from a shore station. At this base a television monitoring system kept the aquanauts under twenty-four-hour observation. In the event one or both became suddenly ill, quick communication with the surface station was possible with a telephone hookup. Decompression chambers were also on hand in case of an emergency.

Efforts were made to provide the sea-floor inhabitants with as many comforts of the land world as possible. Hot meals were brought down to them in pressure cookers; a television set, radio, and library provided entertainment. Fresh hot water for showers was piped down from a support ship on the surface. Twice a day doctors went below to check on the aquanauts' physical condition.

At the end of their week's stay in Conshelf I, the aquanauts rose to the surface none the worse for their experience. Jacques-Yves Cousteau, elated with the success of the experiment, immediately plunged into plans and preparations for a more ambitious undersea dwelling, Conshelf II.

The historic establishment of this dwelling, carried out in June 1963, took place in the warm waters of the Red Sea. The habitat was erected on a submerged reef 25 miles northeast of Port Sudan. Compared with Conshelf I, Cousteau's second undersea-dwelling experiment was really a colonizing effort. It involved building four large steel structures underwater. There was a main dwelling, a garage for the Diving Saucer submersible, and a shed for storing tools and the submarine scooters that the aquanauts rode on their underwater trips. These buildings were anchored on a coral ledge 36 feet down. The fourth structure, called Deep Cabin, was secured at a depth of 90 feet by two lead-filled boxes and was used for experimental deep-diving tests. Several fish pens and anti-shark cages completed the Conshelf II colony.

The main house, a prefabricated structure like the others, was in the form of a central hub and four radiating extensions. To the aquanauts it looked like a starfish, and they named it Starfish House. Five adjustable legs supported the undersea shelter as it rested 7 feet above the floor of the reef. Thus Starfish House was level, even though the reef sloped.

The central hub of the main house was the control center. Here were communications equipment and instrument cabinets. Gauges monitored such items as temperature, air pressure, and the purity of the interior air. Special clocks were set to time the departure and return of divers working outside Starfish House. Three closed-circuit television screens gave the occupants of the control center an overall and continuous view of the activities in and around Conshelf II. One screen pictured happenings in Deep Cabin, a second showed what was going on aboard the surface support ship, and a third televised activities in the sea outside Starfish House. The control center was also the place where the aquanauts ate their meals and relaxed.

The radiating arms leading from the control center were used for sleeping quarters, laboratory work, a darkroom for processing film, a kitchen, and a ready room where the aquanauts put on rubber suits and breathing equipment for excursions into the sea. They left and reentered through an opening in the floor of the ready room. Because the air pressure inside the room was equal to the outside sea pressure, water could not bubble up through the opening.

Attached to this divers' entryway was a circular

anti-shark cage made of strong steel bars. After climbing down a ladder from the opening of the ready room, the scuba divers would pause momentarily inside this cage. They would look around carefully to see if any deadly sharks were in the vicinity. If all was clear, they swam out through a gateway. The cage also provided a protective haven for divers to scurry back to if sharks suddenly appeared.

The garage for the DS-2, the Diving Saucer, was an umbrella-shaped structure. It was open at the bottom so that the small submarine could enter and leave easily. The air pressure inside the garage was maintained at the equivalent of the outside water pressure, keeping the water level down and forming an air-filled chamber above it. The sea garage was not merely a shelter but a well-equipped base from which the submersible could sally forth on exploratory journeys. This was the first time that an underwater structure was used for housing and servicing a submarine.

Deep Cabin was a cylindrical steel dwelling, the interior of which was divided into two levels. Living quarters for two aquanauts occupied the upper level. The lower compartment was used for diving gear and tools, and it also contained an open hatch to the sea.

The main structures of the Conshelf II colony were linked together by closed-circuit television, intercom, telephone, and ultrasonic underwater wireless. The entire undersea colony was connected to the *Rosaldo,* a surface ship that supplied compressed air and electric power by means of hose and cable. Television and telephone hookups completed the link between the undersea colony and the world above.

The deck of a surface support ship is a cluttered, busy place. (Ocean Systems, Inc.)

Cousteau's objective in building Conshelf II was to find out how well a group of aquanauts, in this case five, could live and work beneath the sea for a period of one month. If the Conshelf II experiment proved successful, then Cousteau believed that similar manned undersea stations could be erected for exploiting the riches of the continental shelf anywhere in the world.

Aside from the television and telephone communications, the only breaks the inhabitants of Conshelf II had in their daily undersea routine were periodic visits from the expedition's doctor and colleagues from the surface ship. Boredom was no problem for the aquanauts. They were given a full schedule of work assignments and underwater tests to carry out. One job that kept Conshelf II inhabitants busy was a daily scrubbing of the outer walls of Starfish House and the garage. This was necessary in order to remove the marine growth that formed quickly on steel surfaces. Collecting marine specimens for the expedition's biologist was another chore that took a good deal of time. With the help of fine mesh nets and plastic bags live fish were caught and placed in pens until ready for laboratory study.

A vital part of the Conshelf II experiment was to determine the effects of extreme depths on aquanauts. The tests were made by two aquanauts who lived in Deep Cabin for a week. With scuba gear they made repeated dives to 165-foot depths and worked there without experiencing any difficulties.

A diver's lungs are the first organs of his body to feel the effects of sea pressure at extreme depths. Body tissue is the last to be affected, and it generally does not suffer until really great depths are reached. Breathing a mixture of oxygen, nitrogen, and helium under a pressure of almost four atmospheres (58.8 pounds per square inch), the Deep Cabin aquanauts experienced no unusual respiratory difficulties. Their successful dives indicated that it was entirely safe for aquanauts to remain and work at extreme depths providing they were properly prepared and breathing a suitable air mixture. Furthermore, the tests showed that if aquanauts carried on their deep-sea activities from an underwater base it was better than starting directly from a surface support ship.

Cousteau considered the Conshelf II expedition a success, as was his first underwater living experiment. Man had lived and worked beneath the sea far longer than had previously been thought possible. Cousteau and his colleagues were now convinced that, when properly equipped and housed, man would have little difficulty inhabiting the sea floor. They further believed that permanent manned underwater stations could become practical realities by the mid-1970's. Eager to hasten these developments, Cousteau embarked on still a third undersea expedition in September 1965.

Conshelf III involved five aquanauts who lived at a depth of 328 feet for twenty-one days. Their spherical underwater shelter was 20 feet in diameter and was divided into two levels. The lower level had sleeping quarters, toilet facilities, and storage space for the diving equipment. The aquanauts ate their meals and relaxed in the upper chamber, which was also the communications center. The Conshelf III habitat was anchored to the floor of the Mediterranean Sea just outside of Monaco harbor.

One of the significant activities of the aquanauts was to build an experimental oil-drilling rig. The success of this project proved that it was entirely practical to construct such installations for profitably extracting oil from the sea floor.

Cousteau's theories and predictions concerning manned underwater bases were further supported by the successful testing of similar structures in America. One of the more unusual was an inflatable rubberized shelter created by Edwin A. Link, designer of the *Deep Diver* submersible. Called the Submersible Portable Inflatable Dwelling (SPID), Link's undersea house could be lowered to the bottom of the sea in a collapsed form, then inflated with air to provide a completely pressurized, dry shelter. Weights suspended on chains from the underside of the structure kept it permanently anchored to the sea floor when inflated. An entrance hatch in the bottom of the chamber permitted divers to leave and return on undersea exploring trips.

SPID was successfully tested in June 1964 in the tropical waters surrounding the Bahama Islands. Two aquanauts, Jon Lindbergh and Robert Stenuit, lived in the ocean-bottom habitat for forty-nine hours at a depth of 432 feet. Once inside the underwater shelter the aquanauts rested, ate, and

A scuba diver working on an underwater oil-drilling installation. (Westinghouse Corporation)

slept without experiencing any special problems. From time to time they left the habitat for short sea excursions. Their achievement set a record for deep-sea living at that depth.

Another Link invention, a pressurized diving chamber, was used to transport the divers from a surface ship to the undersea station and back up again.

As a result of the SPID's successful tests, Link feels that his undersea habitat offers certain advantages over the more rigid steel and fiberglass types. The convenience of transporting the lightweight collapsed shelter aboard ship to the area where it is to be lowered into the sea is an important one. Also, it is less difficult and hazardous to anchor to the bottom of the sea. Link believes that wherever divers may be engaged in underwater operations for prolonged periods, SPID can serve as a dry shelter from their labors.

SPID was not Edwin Link's first underwater dwelling. In September 1962 he built a small seafloor shelter that was occupied by a single aquanaut. He lived in the experimental structure for one day at a depth of 200 feet off the coast of France.

Probably the most ambitious experiments in the development of manned undersea stations have been the Sealab projects sponsored by the United States Navy. They were first brought into existence largely through the efforts of Captain George F. Bond. A trained physician, Captain Bond was attached to the Naval Medical Research Laboratory at New London, Connecticut, where he specialized in submarine medicine.

Captain Bond's research was mostly concerned with the medical aspects of deep-sea diving techniques. He conducted detailed studies of new breathing-gas mixtures and diving-time limitations.

In the course of this work the naval officer made the important discovery of "saturation" diving. This means that when a diver breathes a particular gas mixture (such as helium-oxygen) under pressure for a prolonged period, about twenty-four hours, all the tissues of his body become completely saturated with the gas. The diver's body will also be totally pressurized equivalent to the sea pressure at the depth he is swimming. Once the diver has made this adjustment, he is able to remain at the saturation point for an indefinite length of time. This means that his needs for decompression should be based on the depth at which he has been working —as is now done, as a result of Captain Bond's studies—rather than on the length of time he has spent beneath the sea, as was the case previously. A saturated diver, for example, conditioned to work at a depth of 300 feet, requires the same decompression time (about two and a half days) whether his bottom time has been one day or one month.

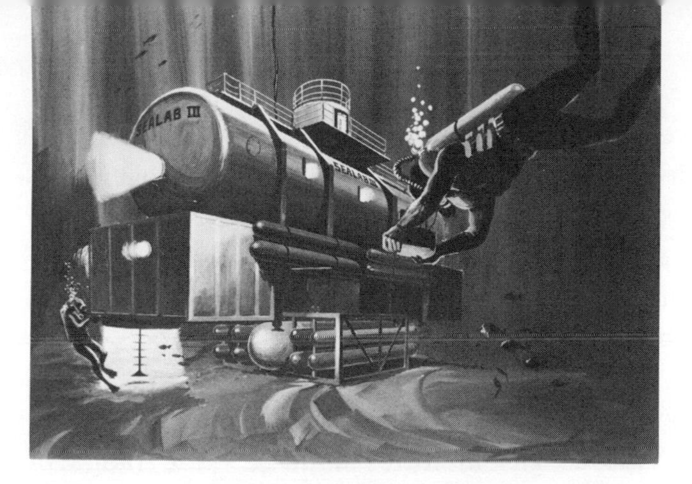

An artist's drawing of Sealab III anchored on the floor of the ocean. (U.S. Navy)

Also important, a saturated diver can retreat to an undersea habitat for rest and relaxation providing the air within the shelter is maintained at the same pressure as the water in which he has been working. Saturation diving greatly increases the time a diver may spend doing useful work on the sea bottom as compared to the time he must spend in decompression. Jacques-Yves Cousteau and Edwin A. Link adapted and refined the saturation-diving technique for their undersea activities.

Captain Bond's research activity made him an enthusiastic oceanographer. Like Cousteau, he believes that if man is to exploit the underwater wealth of the oceans, it will be necessary for him to enter the undersea world and be able to remain there for long periods to explore, observe, build, and harvest.

Genesis I was the start of the Sealab programs. It was strictly a laboratory experiment, begun and guided by Captain Bond in 1957. The project had two major goals. One goal was the development of new gas mixtures to overcome the problems of oxygen poisoning—which results from breathing even the amount of oxygen contained in normal air under prolonged pressure—and nitrogen narcosis. The other goal was to determine the effects of these new gas combinations on man under prolonged, saturated, pressurized conditions. The project was carried out in special chambers at the Naval Medical Research Laboratory, and it was concluded in 1963.

Various gas mixtures under a wide range of pressures were first tried on white rats, guinea pigs, squirrel monkeys, and goats. After careful study of what the animals could and could not tolerate, the next phase of Project Genesis involved tests on human volunteers. This began in November 1962, when three Navy men remained in a pressurized chamber for seven days, breathing an atmosphere of helium and oxygen. They emerged none the worse for their confinement. One effect on the test subjects was a change in their voices. Helium in the gas mixture they breathed caused them to talk with a "Donald Duck" sound.

The tests on human beings reached a climax in August 1963 when another naval team of three men was locked in a pressure chamber for twelve days. The atmosphere consisted of helium, oxygen, and small amounts of nitrogen. The pressure within the chamber was equivalent to that existing undersea at a depth of 200 feet. Successfully demonstrating that certain new gas mixtures, particularly helium and oxygen, could be safely tolerated by man for deep diving, Captain Bond and his associates were now ready to put their findings to actual underwater trials. This led to Project Sealab I.

The Navy's first manned undersea station ex-

Sealab I, the first of the Navy's experimental undersea habitats. (U.S. Navy)

periment was conducted in the clear waters 30 miles southwest of Bermuda from July 20 to July 31, 1964. The habitat used was made from two large steel cylinders taken from an experimental minesweeper boat. The makeshift underwater shelter measured 40 feet in length and 20 feet in diameter and was shaped like an enormous cigar. Two 12-inch portholes were built on each side of the chamber. The interior was crammed with bunks, laboratory equipment, a galley for cooking meals, shower and toilet facilities, air-conditioning equipment, and storage space for scuba gear. The end sections of the undersea station contained water ballast, breathing gas for emergency use, and electrical equipment.

Extending from the habitat to a surface ship was a spaghetti-like tangle of cables for electricity, compressed air, fresh water, a telephone, and a television monitoring system among others. Sealab I was anchored on the ocean floor 193 feet from the surface. It was occupied by four aquanauts, who remained below for the entire length of the experiment without surfacing. The atmosphere of their chamber was composed of 80 percent heli-

Aquanauts adjusting the power and communications cables in preparation for Sealab I's descent to the floor of the ocean. (U.S. Navy)

um, 16 percent nitrogen, and 4 percent oxygen. The air mixture used inside the habitat was one of the important test features of the experiment.

From time to time the aquanauts would leave their habitat, wearing scuba gear, for short exploratory sea journeys or to conduct photographic missions. Two entry hatches in the bottom of the undersea house permitted them to go and come as they wished. It was during a photographic mission that one of the aquanauts suffered the only serious mishap of the experiment.

The incident happened while the submersible *Star I* was visiting the habitat. The vehicle was to perform a series of maneuvers in the vicinity of Sealab I that were to be photographed. While operating his camera one diver suddenly began feeling lightheaded, a sure danger signal. He realized that his scuba was not working properly. The gas supply had somehow been cut off and he was breathing his own exhaled air.

He swam back to the habitat as quickly as he could. But just as he was climbing the stairway to the hatch he collapsed, unconscious. Another aquanaut, on watch inside the station, heard the clanging sound of the stricken diver's air tanks hitting the metal of the shelter. Investigating the noise, he saw the limp body of his colleague drifting away. Quickly swimming to the rescue he grabbed the unconscious aquanaut, pulled him back inside the habitat, and within a minute or so restored him to consciousness and to normal breathing. Except for some ruptured minor blood vessels in the eyes, the aquanaut suffered no other injuries and remained with the experiment to the end.

Unfortunately, Project Sealab I had to be halted before its planned completion date because a hurricane was approaching the test area. Cut short though it was, the experiment was considered a success. The aquanauts suffered no ill effects, physically or psychologically, from breathing the newly created atmosphere. The project produced much new technical information on how undersea stations could be established more efficiently and comfortably for deep-ocean dwellers. Little time was lost in putting this knowledge to work with Project Sealab II, the second stage in the United States Navy's man-in-the-sea program.

To learn more about man's ability to live and work at extreme depths in the sea, the Navy positioned its second manned undersea station 205 feet down off the coast of California. Unlike the Bermuda site, which was especially chosen for its ideal underwater conditions, the second location was selected as a more typical deep-sea environment. Three separate ten-man teams each were to

Sealab II was the second of the U.S. Navy's successful ocean-floor habitats. Thirty aquanauts lived in this station underwater for 15 days at a depth of 205 feet. (U.S. Navy)

live and work underwater for a period of fifteen days. When one team finished its fifteen-day tour, another would replace it. The Project began August 28 and ended October 14, 1965. One of the aquanaut team leaders was Commander M. Scott Carpenter, who had previously gained fame as an astronaut.

Sealab II was a completely new structure, designed and constructed specifically for the job it was to accomplish. The habitat was made of steel and measured 57 feet in length and 12 feet in diameter. Both ends of the station were concave, and midway on its topside there was a conning tower 8 feet in diameter. The undersea station resembled a railroad tank-car without wheels. The conning tower provided the main access to the inside when the habitat was floating on the surface of the sea.

The cylindrical body of Sealab II was fastened to a cradlelike structure made largely of cement for ballast. Additional ballast in the form of lead weights was also carried in this bottom section. The entire undersea station weighed 200 tons.

The interior of Sealab II was divided into four areas. Its stern end contained a hatch that was used by the aquanauts when the station was anchored to the sea floor. Here, too, were shower stalls and space for stowing swim gear. Forward of this compartment was the laboratory, with a built-in sink, cabinets, the breathing-gas control panel, a communications station, and various other installations. Next came the galley and the major portions of the air-conditioning system. The living area for ten aquanauts was in the bow of Sealab II, where there was also an emergency escape hatch.

The most advanced breathing-gas mixture for deep diving was used inside the Sealab habitat. It was composed of helium, nitrogen, and oxygen. The atmosphere was kept at a pressure equivalent to the sea pressure outside the dwelling. The gases in the atmosphere were replenished from banks of cylinders fixed to the outside of the habitat. These, in turn, were refilled from a surface support ship by means of a hose. The mother ship and Sealab

Aquanauts aboard Sealab II at work in the habitat's laboratory area. (U.S. Navy)

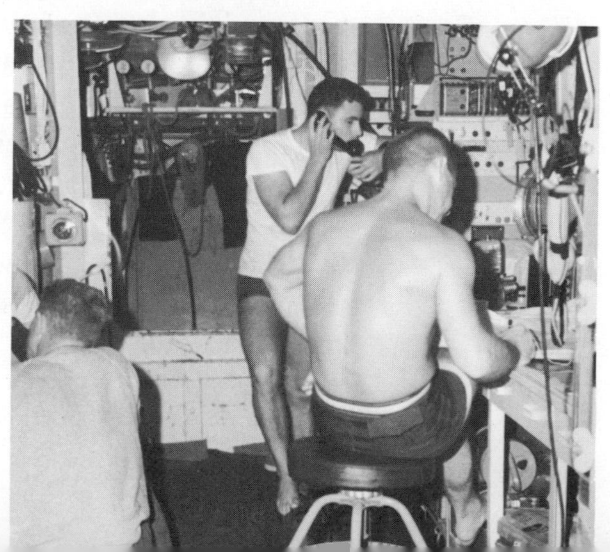

II were also connected by a communications cable, a compressed-air hose, and a cable for alternate electric power. The main electrical power supply for operating the equipment of the habitat came from a shore base. And it was from here also that fresh water was sent down by means of a flexible vinyl pipe.

Sealab II was much like Cousteau's Conshelf II expedition in that it resembled a colony. More than one structure was built. In addition to the habitat itself there was nearby a small, unmanned, automated electronics unit called the benthic laboratory. Housed in an oil-filled inverted steel container, this unit was hooked up by a single coaxial cable to a control console a mile distant on shore. The benthic laboratory served as a kind of electronic traffic controller for the television, audio communication, and numerous telemetering channels between Sealab II and the shore base.

Also near Sealab II was another small structure housing an underwater weather station. The existence of such a unit may sound unusual but it supplied the aquanauts with information vital to their well-being. This included the speed of the underwater currents (comparable to wind velocity above surface), the direction of the currents, the water pressure, the temperature of the sea environment, and the degree of intensity of the light.

Another colony unit was the hulk of an old airplane, on which the aquanauts practiced salvage work. New tools for underwater use and new salvage-work techniques were tested on it.

Still other units in the Sealab II project were a diving bell and a "dumbwaiter" device for hoisting and lowering supplies and equipment to and from the surface ship.

An important physical link between the undersea station and the surface was the Personnel Transfer Capsule (PTC). It served as an elevator for the aquanauts. The Capsule was basically a compression chamber 6 feet in diameter and 11 feet high. The air pressure inside was maintained close to the pressure existing at the 200-foot depth of the habitat. Aquanauts returning to the surface would enter the Capsule through an entry hatch. All ten divers could squeeze their way inside at the same time. Hoisted to the deck of the support ship, the Capsule would then be mated to a decompression chamber. The aquanauts would transfer to this larger and more comfortable compartment to undergo gradual decompression. The process of adjusting divers' bodies to the air pressure at sea level lasted about thirty hours, or until their body tissues were free from the special gas mixture they had been breathing.

The reverse of this process was employed when the aquanauts descended to the Sealab habitat. Locked in the compression chamber they would

A drawing of one model of a Personnel Transfer Capsule (PTC), an elevatorlike unit that transports aquanauts between the surface and their underwater station. (U.S. Navy)

breathe the special atmosphere used in the habitat below while the pressure was increased to that existing at a depth of 200 feet. When their bodies were properly saturated and pressurized with the breathing gas, the aquanauts transferred to the Capsule and were lowered below.

The surface support ship *Berkone* used with Project Sealab II was a vital element in the success of the expedition. It was the command center for the entire operation. Made of two barges connected at one end by a covered platform, the U-shaped vessel was 110 feet long and 90 feet wide. The *Berkone*'s deck was a complex of cranes, compression chambers, medical and communications areas, wires, piping, and tubes. In addition to lowering Sealab to its underwater station, the support ship's personnel carefully monitored every moment the aquanauts spent on the floor of the ocean.

On the morning of August 28, 1965, ten aquanauts of the first team put on their scuba gear and descended to their ocean-floor home. Once inside the Sealab station the men set up house and established communications with the support ship above. One notable event that occurred during the early days of the experiment was the establishment of a live radio link with a Gemini spacecraft then in flight. Aquanaut Scott Carpenter, at 205 feet

A cutaway drawing of a Deck Decompression Chamber. A Personnel Transfer Capsule is shown attached to the top. (U.S. Navy)

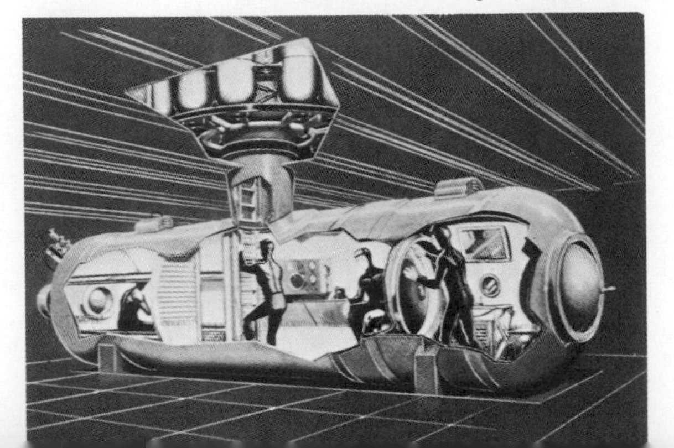

This Personnel Transfer Capsule, dangling from the steel cable, transported teams of aquanauts between Sealab II on the ocean floor and the deck of the support ship Berkone. *(U.S. Navy)*

beneath the sea, spoke to astronaut Gordon Cooper, whose spaceship was orbiting the earth at altitudes from 106 to 217 miles.

The Sealab inhabitants were occupied continuously during their underwater stay. Housekeeping chores; cooking; cleaning; repairing diving lights, pumps, and gauges; and checking scuba gear left little time for relaxation. These activities, however, were secondary to the main tasks: conducting scientific studies and evaluating new equipment.

Sealab aquanauts tested tools and techniques to be used in salvaging sunken wrecks; performed underwater mining studies with experimental tools and methods; collected data—such as current speed, temperature, and water clarity—about their ocean environment; studied fish life; and

Aquanauts testing newly developed electrically heated wet suits. (U.S. Navy)

tested experimental diving suits. Several of their rubber swimsuits were heated electrically so that their bodies could withstand prolonged immersion in cold water.

Tuffy provided some of the more pleasurable moments during the Sealab experiments. Tuffy was a porpoise especially trained to work with the aquanauts. Part of the Sealab experiment was to determine whether this intelligent creature could be of real assistance to men working beneath the sea.

Two difficulties encountered by deep-diving aquanauts are poor visibility and a sense of disorientation as they swim around. Ranging too far from an underwater habitat can be dangerous because the diver may not be able to find his way back. To prevent any such incident during the Sealab experiment the aquanauts were attached to their dwelling by guide lines whenever they swam for any distance. Tuffy was their other safety measure.

Confined to a penned area on the surface of the sea, Tuffy was trained to wear a harness and to respond to a buzzer signal. In a make-believe rescue effort, the porpoise would dive down to the habitat when a buzzer rang. An aquanaut would attach a line to one of the rings on Tuffy's harness, then turn off the buzzer at the habitat. A second aquanaut, pretending to be lost, would then signal the porpoise by turning on his own buzzer. After Tuffy reached the "victim," the aquanaut would remove the line from Tuffy's harness and use it as his guide back to the habitat.

Tuffy was a complete success. His high intelligence made training easy. Once trained, he performed with precision and reliability. In addition to performing the rescue assignment Tuffy proved to be a fine messenger, carrying notes and tools between the surface support ship and the habitat. There was little doubt in the minds of those who participated in Sealab II that porpoises when properly trained can play a vital role in man's future underwater living activities, whether for experimental purposes or more practical endeavors.

Tuffy the porpoise training to rescue "lost" Sealab II aquanauts. (U.S. Navy)

A wild sea lion that wandered into the Sealab area became an unexpected participant in the animal-use test. Named Moki, the creature was trained to respond to a buzzer just as Tuffy was. Indeed, the sea lion showed that it could be as easily trained to work with man as a porpoise.

At the end of the 45-day Sealab II Project twenty-eight Navy men and civilians had spent more than 450 man-days on the ocean bottom. More than 400 man-hours of useful work had been accomplished outside the habitat. To those who had planned and managed Sealab II its success was a long step forward to the time when man will live and work at the bottom of the sea as a matter of course. The United States Navy's third man-in-the-sea experiment, Sealab III, was yet another milestone toward that goal.

Sealab III involved five teams of eight aquanauts each. The aquanauts included both civilian scientists and Navy personnel. Each team was to live in a sea-floor habitat for twelve days. For the first part of the experiment the habitat was anchored at a depth of 450 feet off San Clemente Island, California. Then it was to be moved to a

Moki, a sea lion, also took part in Sealab II's experiments with marine mammals. Tuffy, the main participant, leaps playfully out of the water in the background. (U.S. Navy)

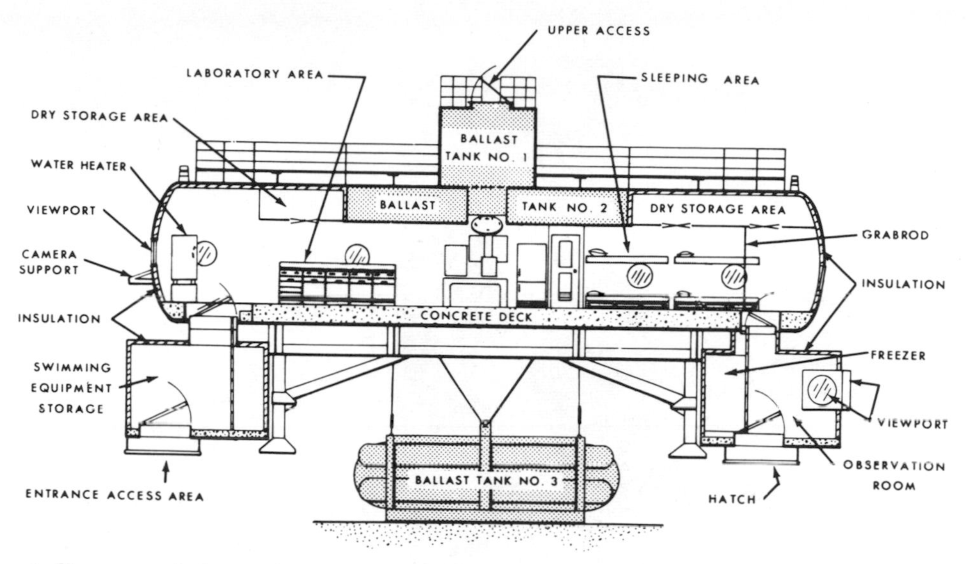

A diagram of the main features of Sealab III. (U.S. Navy)

point 600 feet below the surface of the ocean. The entire experiment was to span sixty days.

The habitat for the Sealab III project was the same as that used for Sealab II, except for the addition of two more rooms, each 8 by 12 feet, to the bottom of the shelter. The room at the stern was a diving station that the aquanauts used when leaving or entering their underwater home. The forward chamber was an observation station and storage compartment. These additions were to provide more living and work space in the main dwelling above. This need was discovered by the aquanauts who took part in Sealab II.

The atmosphere in the Sealab III habitat was the same as that used for Sealab II—helium, nitrogen, and oxygen. However, at the 600-foot level the proportion of gases was to be different, with helium forming 95 percent of the mixture to reduce any danger of nitrogen narcosis. The habitat also contained a device called a "scrubber." This unit held lithium hydroxide, a substance that clears the

For diving in cold ocean waters a warm undergarment is worn beneath this type of wet suit. (U.S. Navy)

interior of bad air by absorbing deadly carbon dioxide. Panels of charcoal were used to absorb offensive odors. Additional apparatus was employed to eliminate carbon monoxide and other dangerous contaminants.

The work program of Sealab III was to include extensive studies of man's physical and mental well-being at extreme ocean depths for prolonged periods. Unfortunately, however, the project was halted before completion, due to the accidental death of one of the participating aquanauts.

An equally important undersea habitat experiment involved four scientists living and working for sixty days at an ocean depth of 50 feet. Operation Tektite, as the project was known, was supported by the United States Navy, the National Aeronautics and Space Administration, the Department of the Interior, and the General Electric Company. The habitat was lowered in the clear, warm waters of Greater Lameshur Bay, Virgin Islands National Park.

The major aims of Operation Tektite were marine-life research and the study of man living in relative isolation in an unfriendly environment. The only contact the aquanauts had with the outside world was limited to telephone communication. For safety and scientific purposes, however, the aquanauts were under constant observation by scientists and doctors on the surface through a closed-circuit television system.

The undersea habitat used in Operation Tektite consisted of two vertical steel structures each 18 feet high and 12 feet in diameter. The two were connected by a tunnel 4 feet wide. The interiors of the chambers were divided into upper and lower compartments for living and working activities. An anti-shark cage was attached to the underside of the sea-floor research station. After dropping through the exit hatch of their shelter, the aquanauts paused behind the protective bars of the cage to see if any menacing sharks were in the vicinity before venturing into the open sea.

The atmosphere within the habitat was a mix-

The undersea station used in Operation Tektite. Note the anti-shark cage at the bottom. (General Electric Company)

The Cachalot *diving system consists of a long decompression cylinder and the smaller transfer chamber on the right. (Westinghouse Corporation)*

ture of oxygen and nitrogen under pressure. The air as well as the drinking water was supplied by hoses linking the habitat with a shore-based support center. Separate cables brought electric power for lighting and communication. A two-month supply of food was stored in the habitat before it was anchored to the sea floor.

In addition to scuba gear for swimming about outside the habitat, the aquanauts also had small, two-man, jet-propelled submersibles for longer field trips.

The interesting project name "Tektite" links the worlds of space and of the ocean. Tektites are small mineral objects, found both on land and in the sea, which have survived a flaming journey through the earth's atmosphere from outer space.

Despite the heavy emphasis on the development of submersibles and habitats in the current undersea program, one of the oldest devices created by

The transfer unit of the Cachalot *diving system. After taking aquanauts to the sea bottom, the chamber may be used as a temporary shelter for the divers when they rest from their underwater tasks. (Westinghouse Corporation)*

man for exploring the bottom of the sea is still in use—the diving chamber. Vastly improved by modern technology, present-day diving chambers are especially valuable for practical undersea work assignments. One modern diving chamber is the *Cachalot*, named for the deep-diving sperm whale. It was developed by the Westinghouse Electric Corporation.

Cachalot consists of two pressure chambers: one remains above the surface on a support ship and is called the deck decompression chamber; the other is the submersible diving chamber. The submersible chamber is used to carry divers from the deck chamber to the underwater work area. Divers preparing to go below first enter the deck chamber. Slowly their systems are saturated with the gas mixture they will breathe undersea, while the air pressure is increased to equal the water pressure encountered at a particular working depth. The deck chamber is equipped for eating, sleeping, and just relaxing while the divers wait patiently for the completion of the compression procedure.

When fully saturated and properly pressurized, the divers step into the diving chamber, which is attached to the deck chamber by an airtight seal. Uncoupled from the latter and sealed off by a hatch cover, the diving chamber is lowered into the water by means of a crane. On the way down, the men put on their diving suits and breathing apparatus. When they reach the working depth the hatch is opened. Because the air pressure inside the chamber is equal to the pressure of the sea outside, water cannot come through the opening.

Dropping through the hatchway into the sea, the divers then connect their breathing apparatus to a "hookah" line that supplies them with the correct gas mixture, generally oxygen-helium. This mixture is stored in steel cylinders fastened to the outside of the diving chamber.

Connected to this "hookah" line is a telephone cable, and a hose through which warm water flows. *Cachalot* divers wear special diurene wet suits, developed by Westinghouse marine engineers, that constantly circulate warm water over their bodies. This allows them to stay below in cold water far longer than if they wore conventional wet suits. Depending on the depth, they can stay in cold water as long as five or six hours—as compared to about an hour at the most in an unheated suit.

During the course of the undersea job aquanauts may rest from their labors from time to time, or have lunch, simply by swimming back to the diving chamber with its dry, warm interior. At the end of the work day, which may last as long as

This newly developed diurene diving suit circulates warm water over a diver's body. This permits him to stay for longer periods in the cold depths of the ocean. (Westinghouse Underseas Division)

six hours, the men seal themselves in the diving chamber, which is then hoisted back to the deck of the support ship. Here the two *Cachalot* chambers are joined by an airtight seal. Still saturated and pressurized, the divers transfer to the larger deck chamber. After a good night's sleep and a hearty breakfast the following morning, the aquanauts are lowered into the sea for another day's work.

If, for example, a job were being performed at a depth of 200 feet, ordinary scuba divers operating from a ship could not remain on the scene for much more than a half hour. Every time they came up they would have to undergo the lengthy decompression process. Aquanauts using the *Cach-*

This aquanaut, busy at an underwater task, was brought to the work area by the Cachalot *transfer chamber in the background. (Westinghouse Underseas Division)*

alot system with its extended submergence technique need not undergo decompression more than once a week. Even this is necessary only in order for them to have weekends off. They can remain on the job with their bodies saturated and pressurized with a gas mixture until the task is finished.

Developers of the *Cachalot* diving-chamber system feel that it is a valuable contribution to man's efforts to live and work at the bottom of the sea. From the standpoint of safety and efficiency, the diving chamber has proved itself on numerous tough, everyday underwater jobs. The ability of divers to work for prolonged periods without undergoing periodic decompression means that there is less physical strain on the divers and also helps to reduce the cost of an undersea job.

The *Cachalot* diving system has been used for such varied underwater tasks as removing debris from trashracks on the face of a hydroelectric dam 200 feet below the surface of a lake; salvaging two offshore oil-well platforms wrecked and sunk in the Gulf of Mexico by the fury of Hurricane Betsy in September 1965; and helping to build the undersea sections of a new bridge spanning Narragansett Bay, Rhode Island.

The excellent performance of the *Cachalot* diving system has inspired Westinghouse marine scientists and engineers to develop a more advanced version capable of supporting divers for extended periods at depths to 1,000 feet.

Marine engineers in Italy and Russia have also contributed to the family of modern deep-diving chambers. Created a few years earlier than the *Cachalot* system, both the Italian and Russian deep submersibles are also used in a different manner. The chambers are primarily for study and observation of the underwater environment. For this purpose they have numerous viewing ports. The crews aboard these diving chambers do not leave them once they are on the floor of the sea.

The Galeazzi Butoscopic Turret, as the Italian diving chamber is called, is a tall cylindrical structure made of high-strength steel plates. The interior has room for only one observer. The upper sides and top of the chamber are pierced by fifteen circular portholes of thick, pressureproof glass. The Turret alone weighs close to 1,000 pounds and slightly over 1,600 pounds with its ballast.

The Italian diving chamber is raised and lowered into the sea by means of a strong steel cable and crane. It can be dropped to a maximum depth of almost 2,000 feet but is usually em-

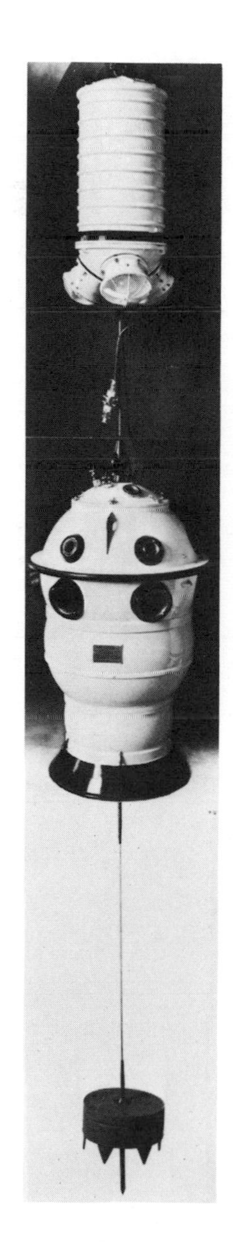

The Galeazzi Butoscopic Diving Chamber. The unit at the top contains lights to brighten the underwater area for observers in the chamber. (Roberto Galeazzi)

ployed at half that depth. A diver using the Turret may stay below for up to three hours.

The GG-57 Hydrostat is one of a series of diving chambers built by Russian engineers. Basically similar in overall appearance to the Butoscopic Turret, the GG-57 is a steel structure that tapers from a large upper cylinder to a small lower cylinder. It stands more than 10 feet high and has a maximum diameter of a little more than 4 feet. With its emergency ballast, this diving submersible weighs 5,000 pounds. The interior of the Hydrostat, which provides about the same amount of space as a public telephone booth, has a revolving bench for one crew member. The arrangement makes it easy to look through five plexiglass portholes placed on all sides of the wall of the chamber.

Like all nonpropelled diving chambers, the Hydrostat is lowered into the sea by means of a crane and steel cable. Its usual operating depth is close to 2,000 feet, although Russian engineers have built in sufficient strength for the submersible to reach 3,000 feet. The air system used within the Hydrostat is capable of keeping its single occupant safe and comfortable for six hours. There are attachments on the exterior of the chamber so that, if necessary, air hoses can be fastened to it from a surface support ship.

In the event of an emergency, the diver aboard the Hydrostat need not wait to be hauled up by means of the cable. He can release the vehicle's ballast, which will cause it to rise to the surface like a cork, because it is positively buoyant.

Used primarily for oceanographic and fisheries research, the GG-57 Hydrostat carries such instruments as five powerful searchlights, depth gauges, still and motion picture cameras, a barometer, and a thermometer.

As man's underwater activities increase in scope and diversity, diving chambers are expected to continue to play an important role.

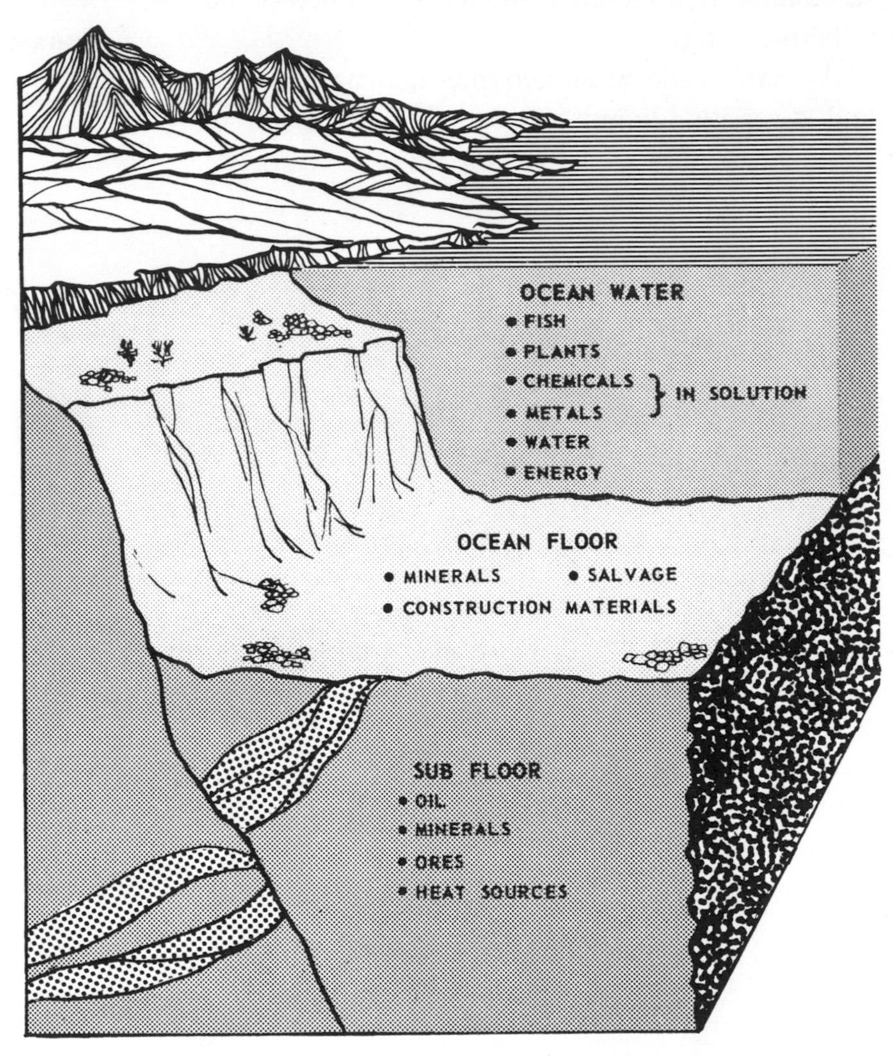

A cutaway chart of the ocean's resources. (Columbus Laboratories, Battelle Memorial Institute)

Chapter 5
Submersibles and habitats of the twenty-first century

Today's submersibles and manned underwater stations are pioneering tools with which scientists and engineers are seeking to explore, study, and develop the ocean depths, the earth's last frontier. The success thus far of underwater research has opened up a world of immense promise for the benefit of mankind. The undersea world of tomorrow will be as exciting and offer as much practical value as man's exploration of outer space.

Experienced underwater explorers and scientists enthusiastically foresee a time, by the twenty-first century or earlier, when improved undersea vehicles and manned ocean-bottom stations will be regularly and widely employed for deep-ocean exploration and research; for exploiting the mineral riches on and below the ocean floor; for expanding the rich food resources of the sea; for underwater transportation; for salvage operations; for the rescue of personnel from any disabled ocean vehicle or underwater settlement.

An artist's concept of what a huge undersea station of the future, exploiting the ocean's food and mineral resources, may be like. (Martin Company, Martin Marietta Corporation)

The fulfillment of these expectations calls for an immense amount of further study and testing by marine scientists and engineers. Progress will be slow and enormously costly. But ultimately, highly efficient undersea vehicles and habitats will be brought into existence. Forces pressing for their creation include: first, man's eternal desire for knowledge of the unknown; second, the great practical worth submersibles and habitats have already demonstrated in deep-sea research; third and perhaps most important, the serious social and economic pressures that mankind is beginning to feel in his limited land environment. The oceans, with their vast resources of food and minerals, have the potential to relieve many of these stresses.

The oceans make up 71 percent of the earth's surface. Yet scientists have barely made a start in their search for knowledge about the deep-ocean environment. This is true even though the modern science of oceanography—a composite research field embracing physics, chemistry, biology, geology, and other sciences—has existed for nearly one hundred years. Oceanography as a science is said to have begun in 1872, when the British ship H.M.S. *Challenger* sailed on a three-year, round-the-world research voyage with a party of scientists.

Future studies of the depths will include detailed explorations and examinations of the ocean floor—its plains, ridges, fissures, trenches, and shelves. Many scientists feel that the secret of the earth's origin is locked in the primeval ooze and rocks lying deep in the oceans. Scientists think that the earth spun from the sun as a cloud of dust and gas an estimated 4.5 billion years ago, and slowly evolved into a solid mass. There were no oceans at the beginning. These came into existence between 100 and 200 million years ago, following periods when the earth experienced cataclysmic upheavals. Thus, in all likelihood, the subterranean layers concealed by the ocean waters contain evidence of the earth as it was countless millions of years in the past. Careful analysis of samples of deeply buried ocean sediments is expected to tell scientists a great deal about the earth's early history.

In the world of outer space a similar effort has been made to determine the origin of the moon from lunar surface samples brought back to earth by Apollo 11 and Apollo 12 astronauts.

Another area of future research will involve an exhaustive study of the living creatures inhabiting the oceans. This is expected to lead to greater understanding of how life originated and evolved on earth. Also, in a more practical sense, man needs to determine the numbers and migratory habits of the thousands of species of fish known to exist in the seas. The outcome of such a study would have important bearing on increasing the supply of food from the oceans.

Other important scientific studies will search for and investigate deep-ocean currents—those moving both horizontally and vertically. Some undersea rivers floating horizontally are thought to move faster than the largest land rivers. Knowing these flow rates will be important for future undersea submarine travel, both for peaceful and military purposes. The vertically flowing currents are known to be closely related to concentrated populations of fish life. For this reason they have aroused a great deal of curiosity among marine biologists.

Tomorrow's submersibles and manned underwater stations will bear the same relationship to today's engineering developments as the modern jet plane bears to the bamboo-and-canvas aircraft first put together by the Wright brothers. Yet their existence will be based on the experience gained from the use of present-day submersibles and habitats.

One future submersible presently in the design stage is the DS-20,000. Engineers of the Westinghouse Corporation who developed the *Deepstar* family of ocean vehicles are building the DS-20,000. This submersible will take scientists nearly four miles down, where they will be able to examine samples of ocean sediments never before seen by man.

One of the first of tomorrow's underwater laboratories is currently in the development stage. It will provide scientists with working and living quarters where they can remain for periods up to thirty days, a mile beneath the ocean surface. This undersea structure is being created by engineers of the Electric Boat Division of General Dynamics for the United States Navy. It is expected to be in operation by the mid-1970's.

The new habitat will consist of two steel cylinders, positioned vertically side by side. The overall size of the structure will be 42 feet long, 48 feet high, and 30 feet wide. One of the cylinders will house the electric power plant for operating the station's equipment. The power plant will receive electric energy from a surface station or support ship by means of a cable.

The other cylinder, maintained as a shirt-sleeve environment, will be the living and working quarters for five scientists. This cylinder will have four levels: one will contain controls for operating the station, two will be devoted to laboratory work, and the fourth will contain living and sleeping quarters.

In the course of their research the scientists will observe the watery environment, either directly through viewports or indirectly through the use of

Scientists will be able to explore four miles beneath the surface of the ocean in submersibles of the future, such as Deepstar 20,000. *(Westinghouse Underseas Division)*

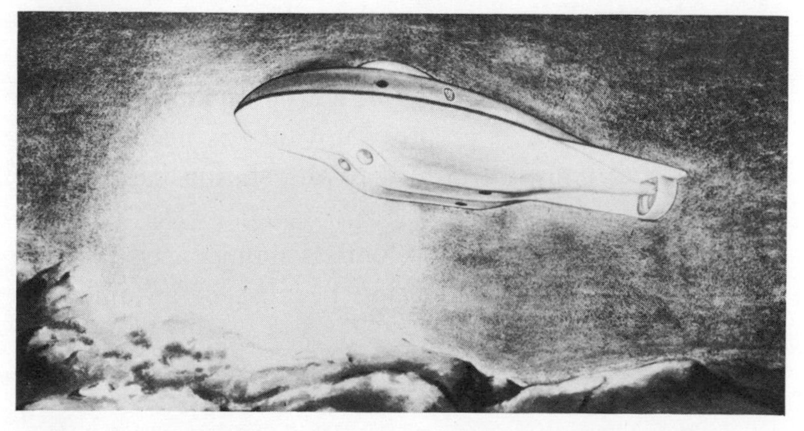

The Navy's future manned underwater station will be anchored to the floor of the ocean. (General Dynamics, Electric Boat Division)

a closed-circuit television system. With a mechanical arm and claw they will collect samples of the ocean bottom or marine life and bring these through a special pressurized entryway into the station for detailed study. Eventually the station may also be equipped with a small, unmanned submersible carrying a television camera. The submersible's movements will be controlled from within the station. It will enable the scientists to study a much wider area around the habitat.

This future underwater station will be supported by four steel legs and held to the ocean bottom by a heavy anchor. The structure will be positively buoyant so that if there is a sudden need for it to rise to the surface its anchor need only be released. If greater buoyancy is needed, additional ballast attached to the station can also be dropped.

In the event the scientists should need to leave their underwater station because of an emergency, a connecting steel sphere between the two cylinders will provide an escape hatchway. The undersea laboratory will also carry emergency life-support and power equipment.

One of the more unusual features of this future station will be a special mating hatch for visiting submersibles. Approaching the station and locking their submersible onto this hatch, personnel will be able to pass through the airtight entryway from sub to station. An ultramodern communications system is being considered that will enable the habitat's scientists to talk to others aboard submerged vehicles, surface ships, and land-based stations and even to receive messages from orbiting satellites.

Other concepts of what tomorrow's fixed underwater stations may be like have been advanced by scientists working with the United States Navy. Strictly in the drawing-board stage, one such station is a tall, steel, cylindrical structure 16 feet in diameter. Its interior is divided into five levels.

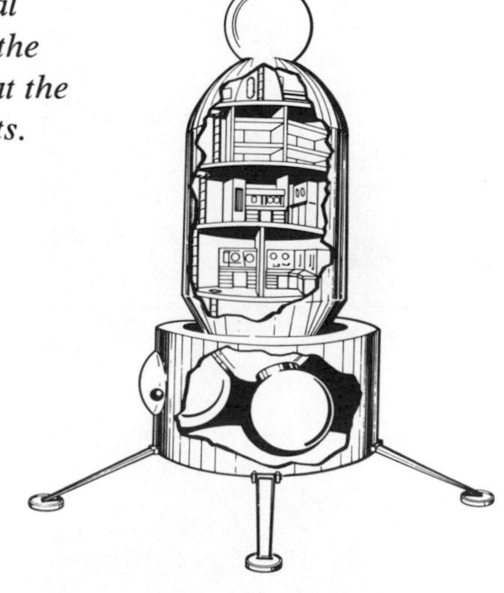

This manned underwater station of the future will have a cylindrical hull. Divers will enter through the sphere at the top. The spheres at the bottom will be observation posts. (U.S. Navy)

A steel sphere attached to the top of the station would be used by aquanauts for entering or leaving. Two additional spheres attached to the bottom of the station would serve as observation points for studying the undersea environment.

Another design for a future undersea habitat would have the shape of a giant doughnut—called a toroid in geometry. It would be erected on a conical base. In outward appearance it would have a close resemblance to some of the wheel-like stations being proposed for outer space. The doughnut-shaped habitat would have an overall diameter of 40 feet and an interior divided into living and working quarters.

Still a third manned habitat proposed by the Navy would consist simply of a giant steel cylinder 20 feet in diameter resting on a diamond-shaped foundation. Fifty feet high, the interior of the station would have two levels devoted to work and living activities.

This future manned underwater station will be built in the shape of a doughnut. (U.S. Navy)

All three of these designs would be for use at depths ranging down to 6,000 feet. Each would be capable of supporting a five-man team of scientists for an indefinite period at a pressure of one atmosphere. Advanced features that set them apart from today's manned deep-ocean stations would include a self-contained power source—most likely a nuclear reactor or a silver-zinc battery unit—and a self-sustaining life-support system independent of any surface source. Food and supplies would be brought by a supply submersible that would attach itself to the station's mating hatch.

The three future habitats would be positioned on the ocean bottom either by a free-descent method or by winching. The free-descent method would require the stations to be weighted until they were negatively buoyant; then they would drop to the sea bottom of their own accord. For the winch-down method, the stations would be constructed to be positively buoyant. Anchors with steel cables and pulleys (sheaves) attached would be lowered first to the bottom of the sea. The cables would pass from the undersea station down through the pulleys, then back up to a winch on the deck of the support ship. As the winch wound up the cables, the undersea station would be hauled slowly to the sea bottom.

Finding out more about the nature of the undersea world will be only one area of research involving tomorrow's underwater vehicles and manned stations. Another equally important area will be the study and exploitation of the oceans' food resources.

Food in the form of fish and plants was the first of the riches man obtained from the seas. Over the course of countless years many of the world's peoples have made seafood a major element in their diets. Many seafoods are rich in vitally important protein. The Japanese, for example, consume a high proportion of seafood, as do many of the people living in the Mediterranean region.

Man's food needs account for a world fish catch of about 110 billion pounds a year. This is an enormous amount measured by any standard. Yet marine biologists say it is really only a fraction of what the ocean is capable of supplying. Out of some 25,000 species of fish, only a handful of different species are actually caught and used for food. This area of oceanography is especially important now because of the world's exploding population and the rapidly increasing difficulty of supplying sufficient food (especially protein-rich food). The seas, with their renewable food resources, should, if properly exploited, help to ease this acute problem.

Before greater advantage can be taken of the ocean's food stock, however, more knowledge must be acquired concerning marine life—edible fish populations in particular. For example, more information is needed about the migratory habits of such fish as tuna, haddock, and salmon. Physical, chemical, and biological data regarding many edible varieties must be collected in order to predict their abundance and distribution. Studies of plankton, the minute plant and animal organisms that fish eat, must be broadened. Further studies of the behavior patterns of various fish are needed, especially of their responses to different kinds of fishing gear.

These and numerous other questions are formidable assignments for the marine biologist. But the research submersible and manned underwater sta-

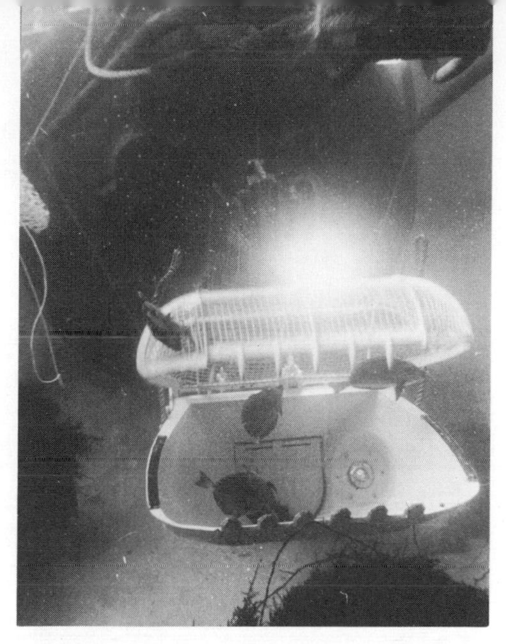

A Japanese submersible uses a special fish-catching scoop to do research in marine biology. (The Yomiuri Shimbun, Japan)

tion are already proving of great value in this work. They bring the scientist directly into the natural environment of the subjects under study.

In addition to marine biologists, commercial fishermen, of course, are also deeply interested in fish studies. Commercial fishing over the past several hundred years has changed little. It is still basically a hunting operation, in which schools of a desired species of fish are tracked down and caught by either hooks or nets.

Present and future underwater vehicles, manned stations, and diving chambers now offer the possibility of radically new fishing methods with the promise of vastly increasing the harvest from the sea. One proposal has been made for the employment of small, tractor-type submersibles dragging trawling nets just above the sea bottom where there are concentrations of fish. The vehicles would have a neutral buoyancy so adjusted that they would travel a few feet above the floor of the sea. Thus they would not disturb or damage the bottom while dragging the nets behind them. The submarine tractors would be guided by scuba divers, much as farmers drive their wheeled tractors on land. Nuclear engines would give these underwater fishing trawlers almost endless operating endurance.

Powerful searchlights mounted on the mini-submersibles would light up the darkness of the fishing area and act also as a lure for fish. A support ship on the surface would constantly track the moving underwater fishermen with sonar and other sensitive detecting devices. When the trawl net was full, the aquanaut fishermen would signal the support ship. Its crew would then lower a hoisting cable and pull up the net full of fish through a hatch opening in the bottom of the boat. The scuba-equipped fishermen who had completed their underwater period of work would also come aboard the mother ship through this hatch. A second team of aquanauts would dive below to continue the trawl operation.

This fishing technique would be practical for ocean depths to 200 feet. This is the present maximum limit at which scuba-divers can remain for any length of time. For the deeper regions of the continental shelf and slope, 600 feet and lower, such underwater fishing operations might be carried on by aquanauts riding comfortably inside deep-water tractor submersibles. Trawl nets might be handled from within the vehicle with the help of mechanical manipulators.

Still another idea for the future involves catcher submersibles equipped with large nets extending on either side. As the vehicles moved through a school of fish, they would be scooped up through the wide open front end of the nets. Small pilot submersibles would be employed with the larger vehicles to locate the fish.

Probably the most imaginative proposal involving underwater vehicles and manned stations for future harvesting of the sea is the creation of fish farms. This involves raising fish within confined areas to assure a steady, maximum production. This is not really a new "fishing" method at all. Aquaculture, as the technique is called, was practiced by the Romans as long as 2,000 years ago. They increased the production of oysters by growing them on ropes in protected water areas. This method is still carried on in many parts of the world, especially in Japan, where it is highly successful. The Japanese also raise squid, which they consider a great delicacy, in this manner.

What makes the modern aquaculture proposal unique, however, is its application to deep-ocean waters and to the gathering of finfish rather than shellfish.

Open-ocean aquaculture would be carried on in areas where nutrients—food on which fish feed—have been artificially concentrated. Marine biologists have learned that in various ocean localities deep, upward-welling currents carry with them enormous quantities of nutrients. Where these occur there is teeming fish life. These upward-moving currents contain nutrients in the form of decomposed remains of organisms that once lived at the ocean's surface. After dying they sank to the bottom. As the decomposed matter is carried up into the sunlit portions of the sea, it stimulates enormous plankton "blooms" or growth. Plankton are tiny sea animals and plants, some so small they consist of just a single cell. Plankton are the basic item in the diet of fish, big and small. Where there is a concentration of plankton, there is sure to be found a gathering of fish. The long-famous fishing banks off Newfoundland are one such locality. In addition to the current that produces these banks, there is another and more recently discovered vertical current off the coast of Peru. One suggestion for creating a vertical-flowing, food-rich current from the ocean floor is to use a nuclear-powered heating device.

Once the artificial current was established, the congregating schools of fish would be restricted to the area. This would be done with the help of devices employing electrical, acoustical, and perhaps even chemical means. All these methods are known to have a strange, hypnotic effect on fish. Another technique would ring the area with a curtain of air bubbles. Marine biologists have found that when columns of air bubbles are created in the sea, fish will not swim through them.

With the help of artificial barriers, aquanaut fish farmers could then tend their marine herds. Depending on the depths at which the fish farms existed, these aquanaut farmers would swim around them and be concerned primarily with chasing away any predators. Fixed shelters on the ocean floor would allow them dry, warm havens in which to relax from their shepherding duties.

If the fish farms were established at depths beyond the range of the scuba divers, men would watch over their marine flocks by riding within miniature submersibles. Dr. Athelstan Spilhaus, a noted American scientist, has advanced the suggestion that underwater shepherds might be aided in their work by specially trained porpoises, performing the way sheepdogs do on land.

Open-ocean fish farms would radically change the present-day fishing industry from that of a hunting activity to one more comparable to herding cattle on land. As with the cattle industry, choice kinds of fish might even be bred for special markets. Harvesting the products of a fish farm would be accomplished with a suction-pipe device leading from the enclosed area directly into a surface ship. This means of catching fish in quantities is already being employed on a limited scale.

Food from the sea also includes plants in the form of algae. For centuries people living along coastal areas have obtained much of their nourishment from seaweed. The Japanese have brought the use of seaweed for human food to its highest development. They cultivate a red alga, *nori,* on nets and bushes planted in shallow waters. As a source of cheap protein for a growing world population, algae cultivation could be intensified and expanded with the help of many of the new tools and methods being developed for increased fish production.

By whatever future means the fantastically rich

Tuffy, the porpoise trained in the Sealab II experiment, proved that intelligent creatures of this kind have great potential for future undersea work. (U.S. Navy)

A digging and loading installation such as this may one day mine ocean-floor minerals. (Engelhard Minerals & Chemicals Corporation)

store of food held by the oceans is exploited by man, there is little doubt that underwater vehicles and manned stations will play major roles in that endeavor.

Mining the mineral treasures of the oceans is yet another activity of the future in which submersibles and habitats will play essential parts. The oceans are thought to contain more minerals than have ever been mined from the land. These mineral riches exist in an almost inexhaustible supply, constantly being renewed by such natural processes as erosion, decay, and runoff from the continental land masses. The same valuable minerals found on land occur in the oceans too. They exist in solution in the ocean waters, lie in deposits on the ocean floor, and are buried in the rocks and sediments beneath the ocean floor.

Man has long extracted mineral riches from the sea. Salt and magnesium from the water, tin and diamonds from shallow offshore deposits, and oil and natural gas from beneath the continental shelves are some of the important minerals now

These ore-rich nodules carpet vast stretches of the ocean floor. (Woods Hole Oceanographic Institution)

being mined. Interest is increasing in minerals that are known to exist in tremendous quantities in the deeper regions of the ocean world.

Not the least of these valuable minerals are ore-rich nodules that cover certain areas of the ocean floor. Consisting mostly of manganese, copper, cobalt, nickel, and iron, nodules are scattered in thick concentration in the Pacific and Atlantic for countless square miles. Nodules were first discovered by members of the H.M.S. *Challenger* expedition in 1872. Little more than curiosities at the time, these black, ore-rich lumps were forgotten for almost a hundred years, until their rediscovery by oceanographers during the International Geophysical Year (1957–1958).

A study of nodules has shown that they actually "grow" in layers, like an onion, as deposits build up on a small center core generally of glass, stone, or clay. Samples brought up from the sea bottom indicate that nodules range in weight from a few ounces to several tons. Their growth rate has been estimated as one millimeter in a thousand years. This is fantastically slow, but so many of them are in a continuous state of accumulation that they could be an inexhaustible resource to supply man's mineral requirements. It has been estimated that one square mile of nodule-covered ocean floor could yield 6,000 tons of manganese, 4,000 tons of iron, and 125 tons of copper, cobalt, and nickel.

A number of ideas have been advanced for the recovery of ore-rich nodules. One scheme would use an underwater vehicle equipped with a vacuum-cleaner device that would suck them up. They would pass upward through a giant tube to a surface cargo ship. Conceivably, they might also be piped directly into a giant submarine cargo-carrier, which would then transport them to a land-based extracting and smelting plant. Another idea involves the use of an unmanned, underwater vehicle whose ore-recovery operations would be controlled from a surface ship.

It is known that the geologic rock and sediment formations of the sea bottom are much the same as those of the earth's land areas. This has led to the belief that the regions below the sea floor must contain deposits of the same minerals found beneath the land masses. The underwater vehicle, equipped with sensitive detecting devices, could serve as the ideal tool for exploring and surveying potentially rich mineral areas.

If such ore deposits were found near a seacoast, shafts could be sunk on land and tunnels bored toward the ore bed beneath the sea. Coal is being recovered from underwater mines of this type in Great Britain, Japan, and other countries.

For mineral deposits lying many miles from shore and at a great depth beneath the floor of the sea, it is anticipated that large structures could be built over the site, completely watertight and pressurized. Using the same techniques, tools, and equipment required for mining on land, shafts could be sunk into the ore bed and tunnels dug. The installation could be equipped with a series of air locks for the movement of men and supplies and the removal of the extracted ore to underwater cargo-carriers. This deep-ocean mining habitat would have facilities for the miners to eat, sleep, and relax after their workday was completed. The miners might work for a week or two, then return aboard a small transport submarine to a surface shore base. Their places would be taken by a relief crew. One end of the mining structure would have a special air lock for docking the submarine transport.

Undersea vehicles would be vitally important to such a mining installation—carrying supplies, construction materials, tools, equipment, and men. They would also serve as ore carriers or submarine tugs, hauling a series of specially designed barges filled with ore to a land-based extracting plant.

Before the exploitation of solid mineral ores from deep-ocean regions becomes a reality the first mineral riches taken from the sea will be oil and natural gas. These valuable carbon fuels are already being removed from the sea floor on an ever-increasing scale. As the world's demand for them grows, underwater deposits are being exploited more and more. In shallow areas of the continental shelves a number of rich oil and natural gas pools have been found. Some places where pools are now being vigorously exploited include the Gulf of Mexico region off the coast of the United States, the waters off southern California, and—one of

A drawing of an undersea oil field of the future. Inflated buoyancy spheres on the left support the oil-drilling equipment; a cargo submarine tows flexible bags containing petroleum products; the wheel-shaped units are flexible storage tanks for refined fuel; the small structures with pointed legs are the homes of workers; the oil refinery is under the domed structure on the right. (Reynolds Metals Company)

the newest discoveries—certain sections of the North Sea off the coasts of England and Holland.

Drilling towers with long, steel legs anchored on the sea floor are currently used to extract oil and natural gas from beneath the sea. As the search for these minerals proceeds into deeper waters, specially rigged ships will be employed for the drilling operations. However, as oil exploration and exploitation advance to the very deepest regions, underwater vehicles and manned installations appear to be the only practical means of operating. Experts in the petroleum industry feel that this future deep-sea activity will be in progress by the mid-1970's.

Future oil surveying and drilling activities on the deep-ocean floor will almost certainly call for the use of a variety of submersibles. They would perform such tasks as exploring and test-drilling for oil, building underwater drilling rigs, and towing oil-filled barges to a land-based refinery.

A typical future ocean-bottom oil field could also have a series of storage facilities for holding surplus petroleum. One of the world's biggest underwater oil-storage tanks has already been constructed and is anchored to the bottom of the Persian Gulf. Serving as a storage and loading depot for an oil field in the Dubai sheikdom, the giant undersea tank weighs 15,000 tons and holds half a million barrels of oil.

Although the economic necessity for exploiting ocean-bottom minerals, especially solid ores, does not yet exist—nor do the technological means for obtaining them—the day is not far off when these will become actualities. The fast depletion of the nonrenewable mineral resources on land almost certainly will force man to turn to the oceans' riches to satisfy his requirements.

When the first practical submarines were created they were considered solely as instruments of naval warfare. Little thought was given to their possible use as cargo-carriers. The only exception to this was during World War I and World War II. A small number of undersea boats were employed by Germany and Japan for transporting petroleum, certain scarce metals, and other items of military importance. Now, with all the modern technological developments being applied to undersea vehicles, especially nuclear propulsion systems, there is new and vigorous interest in adapting submarines for commercial transport purposes.

Commercial submarines would have several advantages over surface freighters. For one thing, submarine cargo-carriers would not have to contend with bad weather and sea conditions. They

A drawing of a new salvaging method being developed by the Navy. The system will be able to raise objects weighing up to 1,000 tons from depths as great as 850 feet. (U.S. Navy)

would experience no delays while traveling serenely in the depths of the sea. Furthermore, submarine transports could take advantage of shorter global routes between continents. For example, their ability to sail beneath the north polar ice cap would shorten the journey between New York and Tokyo by close to 2,000 miles. An even shorter distance would be realized for commercial submarines voyaging between Tokyo and London.

Future commercial submarines might be giant vessels, ranging up to 100,000 tons in size. They might be designed to carry either a liquid cargo like petroleum, or a dry cargo. With special hull designs and advanced propulsion systems, these cargo-carrying submarines of the twenty-first century could travel at speeds of up to 200 knots.

Another proposal for a future underwater cargo-carrier visualizes a powerful submarine that would perform as a tugboat hauling a string of barges. The latter would be made of some flexible, waterproof material and would travel linked together nose to tail, like a string of sausages. Such an underwater transport system would be particularly well-suited for moving liquid cargoes.

Future cargo submarines may also bring into existence undersea port facilities. Sliding into special air locks, submarines could be loaded or unloaded and even serviced at these stations. Undersea port facilities would be particularly good for coastal localities where it is not possible to build good port installations on the land. Underwater docking stations would also offer protection to cargo submarines during periods of storm.

Salvaging the cargoes of sunken ships is one of the oldest of man's underwater activities. Indeed, the desire to retrieve sunken treasure was the chief inspiration for the creation and development of some of the earliest diving equipment.

Salvage work is one of the most difficult and costly of undersea operations. But modern deep-diving submersibles, scuba gear, and the many new tools and instruments for undersea use have done much to improve the picture. The future of salvage work has an enormous potential for commercial gain. Many salvage prizes still lie at the bottom of the sea ready for the taking.

Ever since man began sailing the oceans, thousands of vessels have gone to the bottom, mainly as the result of storms and warfare. During the sixteenth century fleets of Spanish galleons were used to bring back treasure the conquistadores took in their conquests of the Inca and Aztec empires of South and Central America. Many of these wooden ships, laden with gold, silver, and precious stones, never made it to Spain. As a result, much of the floor of the Caribbean Sea is a treasure trove of wrecks. By means of scuba gear and in some instances submersibles, a number of these old Spanish wrecks have been found and some of their valuable cargo recovered.

There are equally valuable wrecks of more modern vintage that offer salvage workers unlimited financial rewards. The vast majority of these sunken ships were victims of deadly submarine warfare during World Wars I and II.

Locating a sunken ship is one of the most difficult phases of salvage work because of the vastness and irregularity of the ocean floor. Generally, surface ships "drag" a specific bottom area with cable-suspended hooks or electronic detecting devices. It is a hit-or-miss procedure that more often than not ends with zero results.

Undersea vehicles promise to improve these search techniques enormously. They have the ability to travel close to the ocean floor and can use such specialized equipment as sonar, television, and powerful searchlights for visual inspection. The *Trieste* demonstrated the advantages of underwater vehicles for search activities when it found the remains of the submarine *Thresher* after scores of surface salvage ships had failed.

Bringing scuba divers directly to the scene of a wreck will be another important contribution by submersibles to future salvage operations. Diving chambers that serve as temporary underwater shelters for aquanauts working at salvage tasks will also play a vital role.

When wrecks lie at depths beyond the range of scuba divers or hard-hat aquanauts, specially constructed one-man submersibles are foreseen that will perform the needed tasks. These vehicles will have highly dexterous manipulators for handling wrenches, cutting torches, and other tools that the salvage worker will operate from within.

Many of the same technical developments to be used for salvage work may well be applied to the field of marine archaeology. This specialized branch of archaeology is concerned with finding and studying the remains of past civilizations that lie buried beneath the sea.

Jacques-Yves Cousteau and his colleagues have demonstrated the valuable help modern equipment can give to this fascinating science. They have located the wrecks of some Greek and Roman ships that have been lying on the floor of the Mediterranean Sea for more than 2,000 years. Well-preserved amphorae—vases for holding wine and olive oil—and other relics of ancient times have been brought to the surface. Archaeologists from the University of Pennsylvania, using the submersible *Asherah,* have made even more important underwater discoveries.

Ancient sunken ships, and "lost cities" that have slipped beneath the sea as the result of earthquakes or tidal waves, will be more accessible in the future to marine archaeologists riding within submersibles and wearing modern diving gear. In many instances such underwater finds will tell more about past civilizations than similar land sites. Archaeological remains in the sea, although covered by sediments and marine growth, have remained safe from vandalism or from further destruction by natural causes.

It is predicted that when the construction of the small submersible is perfected, it will be widely used for recreational purposes. Just as small private planes have become an offshoot of commercial and military aircraft, pleasure seekers of the future will be using miniature submersibles to "get away from it all" on silent journeys through the undersea world. Safer and more comfortable breathing-gas mixtures and underwater gear will also encourage recreation beneath the sea.

Of course, many people who would not want the expense or trouble of owning their own submersibles might nevertheless wish to visit the unique undersea world. For these individuals there will be sightseeing submersibles, sailing on regular tours through exotic areas. Most of these tour regions will probably be located in warm, clear, tropical waters, such as those off Florida, in the Caribbean, and in the South Pacific. In tropical areas the undersea world is one of exotic splendor, with fascinating reef formations, graceful marine plants, and rainbow-hued fish.

Submarine tours are not just a dream of the future. In 1964 the submarine *Auguste Piccard* was used for this purpose during the Swiss National Exposition at Lausanne. Carrying forty tourists at

In tropical areas the undersea world is often one of great beauty. (J. W. LaTourrette, Wometco Miami Seaquarium)

a time, the *Piccard* took short trips to a depth of 900 feet below the surface of Lake Geneva. This submarine tour proved to be one of the most popular features of the exposition.

Also possible in the future are underwater restaurants and hotel-like shelters. Erected in shallow water, such pleasure shelters would not have the problem of a pressurized atmosphere to bother visitors. In shallow regions the change in pressure would be so slight that no special artificial atmosphere, breathing apparatus, or dress would be required. These underwater pleasure spots might well come into existence as extensions of seaside hotel resorts. Tunnels would provide easy walkway access between the land and undersea structures. Glass or other transparent materials would be used for building the airtight and watertight buildings so all the beauty of the sea environment could be appreciated.

Indeed, the world's first underwater tourist tower has already been built 200 feet offshore from the resort village of Shirahama, Japan. Sixty-four feet high, the submerged half of the tower has viewing ports 5 feet above the sea floor. Two underwater national parks, where scuba divers may enjoy colorful marine life, are also in existence at Key Largo, Florida, and St. John, Virgin Islands.

Many different factors will determine the future advances in underwater vehicles and habitats. Not the least of these are the materials deep-ocean submersibles and structures will be built with. Current technological work on building materials is following two broad avenues: One seeks to improve the qualities of metals already in use—high-strength steels, titanium, and aluminum; the other is trying to find new, superior materials, especially for use at depths of three miles and below.

Most unusual of the new materials under investigation are glass and glass-reinforced plastics. Tests have shown that while these materials have certain undesirable characteristics, they also have good qualities. Their light weight is important for needed buoyancy in a submersible. More valuable still, they have the ability to withstand enormous compression forces when formed into spherical shapes. Being able to withstand the crushing pressures existing at extreme ocean depths is, of course, the chief requirement that any of these new materials will have to meet. Then there is the obvious advantage of far better visibility for crew members than that provided by steel subs with their small portholes.

The first experimental glass submersible has been built at the Oceanic Institute, Oahu, Hawaii. Made of 1⅛-inch-thick plexiglass, the hull, shaped like a ball, measures 53 inches in diameter. Two aquanauts can squeeze inside. The "bubble sub," as it is nicknamed, is driven by three battery-powered outboard motors and can travel at a top speed of 2 knots. It is capable of exploring the underwater world at a maximum depth of 300 feet for as long as four hours.

Man himself may be a more important future factor than materials. At the moment divers using scuba gear cannot remain long at depths below 200 feet. New breathing equipment and gas mixtures now under development are expected to extend the range of free-swimming divers to more than 1,000 feet. Hard-hat divers, who normally do not work at depths greater than 500 feet, will also benefit from these future developments.

The glass research submersible Kumukahi. *With space for two crew members, it has a working depth of 300 feet and a speed of a little more than 1 knot. (Makai Range, Inc.)*

Foreseeing the time when aquanauts might be required to leave their submersibles or habitats to explore at depths of more than 1,000 feet, a far more revolutionary idea than improvements in mechanical breathing apparatus has been proposed. Veteran undersea explorers like Cousteau feel that man may have to undergo physical modification to make him more of an aquatic creature than he is. Special surgical techniques, yet to be determined, may enable man to endure the harsh, hazardous depths of the ocean with almost the same facility as the semi-aquatic seal.

Another idea for modifying man physically involves the use of a special liquid for filling the lung cavities. The liquid would provide the needed oxygen for breathing underwater and at the same time act as a filling or support, to prevent lung damage by compression. Scientists have already demonstrated this possibility experimentally by placing mice in liquid-filled jars under pressures equivalent to those existing several thousand feet down in the ocean. After prolonged immersion and quick return to sea level pressure, the creatures survived without ill effects.

At this point in time it appears that man's future activities in the undersea world will be far-ranging. They will be limited only by his imagination and will to achieve. In a report to the President of the United States, members of the Council on Marine Resources and Engineering Development said: "The time is ripe to apply our knowledge of the sea. To be sure there is much that we still do not know—this will always be true—but we know more of the sea than our actions towards exploitation might suggest. The technology is ready—new structural materials, miniaturized electronics, computers, nuclear power, underwater vehicles. These tools await utilization."

A Glossary of Some Oceanographic Terms

abyss. The term for an extremely deep part of the ocean. It usually means below 300 fathoms (1,800 feet).

acoustics. The science of sound—dealing with its production, transmission, and effects.

algae. A family of sea plants that ranges in size from plants of a single cell to giant kelps 100 feet long. Seaweeds belong to the algae family.

atmosphere. The gaseous envelope of air that surrounds the earth. It is essential to all forms of life. It is composed of 79 percent nitrogen and 21 percent oxygen. Included, too, are small quantities of argon, carbon dioxide, xenon, helium, and other gases.

atmospheric pressure. The pressure of the atmosphere due to the force of gravity. At sea level the air pressure measures 14.7 pounds per square inch.

aquaculture. The raising of finfish and shellfish under controlled conditions within a confined area.

bathymeter. An instrument to measure the depth of the sea.

bathyscaph. Also *bathyscaphe.* A free-moving, manned vehicle used to explore the deepest parts of the oceans.

bathysphere. A steel spherical chamber used by scientists to observe and study ocean depths.

Such chambers are lowered and raised in the sea by means of a winch and a steel cable.

buoyancy. The ability of an object to float on the surface of a fluid or to ascend through and remain freely suspended in a compressible fluid such as seawater.

continental shelf. An undersea zone adjacent to a continent or around an island and extending from the low-water line to an average depth of about 500 feet, where the shelf's bottom drops steeply to the deeper ocean floor. Although it varies widely, this feature of the ocean bottom has an average width of 40 miles.

continental slope. That part of the ocean floor extending from the edge of the continental shelf to the deeper parts of the ocean. On the average it begins at a depth of about 500 feet and inclines steeply to approximately 11,000 feet.

current meter. An instrument for measuring the speed of an ocean current. Some current meters show both direction and speed.

decompression sickness. Also *bends, caisson disease, compressed-air illness*. A condition caused by ascending too rapidly from the sea floor to the surface. This causes gas bubbles to form in the bloodstream or tissues of divers, and—depending on number, size, and location—these bubbles can bring on severe pain, paralysis, unconsciousness, and even death.

echo sounder. An instrument for determining the depth of water. This device finds depth by measuring the time span between the transmission of a sound or ultrasonic signal and its return or echo from the bottom.

fathom. A unit of measure for gauging ocean depths. It is equal to 6 feet (1.83 meters).

helium. An element that occurs as a light, inert, colorless gas, a trace of which is naturally present in our atmosphere.

kelp. A species of usually large, blade-shaped or vinelike brown algae. Since the seventeenth century people have used the burnt ashes of kelp as a source of sodium carbonate, potash, and iodine.

knot. A speed unit of one nautical mile (6,076.112 feet) per hour.

nitrogen. A colorless, tasteless, odorless, nonpoisonous gas that forms almost 79 percent of the earth's atmosphere.

nitrogen narcosis. Also *rapture of the deep*. An intoxicating or narcotic effect produced in divers breathing gaseous nitrogen in compressed-air mixtures at depth for a prolonged period.

oceanography. The study of the sea, including the physical characteristics of seawater, the geology of the land beneath the oceans, the chemistry of seawater, and marine biology.

oxygen. An element occurring as a free gas in the atmosphere and as a combined element in seawater. It is necessary to all plant and animal life.

plankton. Minute organisms drifting or weakly swimming in salt or fresh waters. The plant forms are phytoplankton. The animal forms are zooplankton.

salinity. A measure of the quantity of dissolved salts in seawater.

sea floor. The bottom level of the ocean, where there are generally smooth, gentle slopes.

sediment. Particles of organic and inorganic matter accumulated on the sea floor.

sonar. An abbreviation for the words *so*und *na*vigation *a*nd *r*anging. It refers to the method or equipment for determining by underwater sound techniques the presence, location, or nature of objects in the sea.

trim. A submariner's term to describe a submerged vessel's position with respect to its state of buoyancy and fore-and-aft balance.

Suggested Further Reading

BOOKS

Bardach, John. *Harvest of the Sea.* New York: Harper & Row, 1968.

Carlisle, Norman. *Riches of the Sea: The New Science of Oceanology.* New York: Sterling Publishing Company, 1967.

Carrington, Richard. *A Biography of the Sea.* New York: Basic Books, 1960.

Carson, Rachel L. *The Sea Around Us.* New York: Oxford University Press, 1951.

Cousteau, Jacques-Yves. *The Living Sea,* with James Dugan. New York: Harper & Row, 1963.

———. *World Without Sun,* ed. James Dugan. New York: Harper & Row, 1964.

Cromie, William J. *Exploring the Secrets of the Sea.* New Jersey: Prentice-Hall, 1962.

Dugan, James. *Undersea Explorer: The Story of Captain Cousteau.* New York: Harper & Brothers, 1957.

Marx, Robert F. *They Dared the Deep.* New York: The World Publishing Company, 1967.

Cousteau, Jacques-Yves. "Diving Saucer Takes to the Deep." *National Geographic,* April 1960, pp. 571 ff.

———. "At Home in the Sea." *National Geographic,* April 1964, pp. 465 ff.

Hendrickson, Jr., Walter B. "Rescue from the Deep." *Popular Mechanics,* January 1968, pp. 124 ff.

Interagency Committee on Oceanography. *Undersea Vehicles for Oceanography*. Pamphlet No. 18, October 1965. Available for 65¢ from Superintendent of Documents, U.S. Government Printing Office, Washington, D.C.

Keach, Lt. Cmdr. Donald L. "Down to Thresher by Bathyscaph." *National Geographic,* June 1964, pp. 744 ff.

Link, Edwin A. "Tomorrow on the Deep Frontier." *National Geographic,* June 1964, pp. 778 ff.

Oceanographer of the Navy. *The Ocean Engineering Program of the U.S. Navy*. Alexandria, Va.: Office of the Oceanographer of the Navy, September 1967.

U.S. Naval Oceanographic Office. *Questions About the Oceans*. Publication G-13. Available for 55¢ from Superintendent of Documents, U.S. Government Printing Office, Washington, D.C.

Index

Alexander the Great, 4-5
algae as food source, 151
Aluminaut (submersible), 58-61
Alvin (submersible), 54-58
ama, 2
American Revolution, 16
animal-use tests, 128-130
anti-shark cages, 111, 133
Apollo spacecraft, 145
aquaculture, 155-157
archaeology, 72, 167
Archimedes, 13
Argonaut (submarine), 25
Aristotle, 4
Asherah (submersible), 71-72, 167
August Piccard (submarine), 168-169

ballast systems:
  of submarines, 13, 17
  of submersibles, 52, 66, 82
Barton, Otis, 39
bathyscaphe, 39-48, 166
bathysphere, 39
Beaver Mark IV (submersible), 78-83, 94-95
Beebe, Dr. William, 39
bends, 35-36
Ben Franklin (submersible), 63-69
benthic laboratory, 124
Berkone (ship), 126
Bond, Capt. George F., 116
Bourne, William, 12-14
breathing apparatus, *see* snorkels; scuba
buoyancy, principle of, 13
Bushnell, David, 16-20

Cachalot (diving chamber), 135-139
Carpenter, Commander M. Scott, 122, 126-127
catcher submersibles, 154-155
Challenger (ship), 145, 159
Challenger Deep, 43, 45
Charles V, emperor of Spain, 7
Civil War, 21-23
commercial fishing, 153-155

communications systems of research submersibles, 41-42, 45, 68
compression chambers:
for diving chambers, 135
for habitats, 125-126
computers, 99
Conshelf I, 108-109
Conshelf II, 109-113
Conshelf III, 113-114
Controlled Underwater Recovery Vehicle (CURV), 102-103
control systems on research submersibles, 56
Cook, Capt. James, 44
Cook Deep, 43, 44
Cooper, Gordon, 127
Council on Marine Resources and Engineering Development, 172
Cousteau, Jacques-Yves, 34, 48-50, 53, 108-109, 112-114, 117, 167, 171
Cyane, 3-4

David boats, 21
Da Vinci, Leonardo, 28-29
Davis, Sir Robert H., 107
Day, John, 12
decompression, 82, 116-117
diving chambers and, 135-138
decompression chambers:
for diving chambers, 135
for habitats, 125, 126
Deep Diver (submersible), 83-87
deep-ocean currents, 146
deep-ocean mining, 161
Deep Ocean Work Boat (DOWB), 87-98
Deep Quest (submersible), 90-92
Deepstar 2,000 (submersible), 72
Deepstar 4,000 (submersible), 72-73
Deep Submergence Rescue Vehicle (DSRV-1), 97-101
Deep Submergence Search Vehicle (DSSV), 101-102
Denayrouze, Auguste, 33-34
Department of the Interior, 132
De Son (inventor), 15-16
diving, free, 1-2
diving, saturation, 116-117
diving bells, 7-12
ancient use of, 5
closed, 11-12
open end, 7-11
diving chambers, 135-141
advantages for scuba divers of, 135-138
fishing methods with, 153
research uses of, 139, 140
salvaging uses of, 138-139
Diving Saucer, 48-54, 109, 111
diving suits (*see also* wet suits), 29-33
Drebbel, Cornelis, 14
DS-20,000, 146
dugongs, 62

Eagle (ship), 19
echo sounder, 41-42

fathometers, 88
fish farms, 155-157
fishing, commercial, 153-155

food resources, undersea, 151-158
Franklin, Benjamin, 28, 62-63
free diving, 1-2
frogmen, 5
Fulton, Robert, 20-21

Gagnan, Émile, 34
Galeazzi Butoscopic Turret, 139-140
Gemini spacecraft, 126
General Dynamics Corporation, 71, 147
General Electric Company, 132
General Motors Corporation, 87
Genesis I, 117-118
GG-57 Hydrostat, 140-141
Grumman Submersible Vehicle #1 (GSV-1), 92-94
Gulf Stream Drift Mission, 62-69
Gymnote (submarine), 26

habitats, 107-134
  animal-use tests in, 128-130
  atmosphere used in, 117-118, 122, 131-132, 133-134
  communication between spacecraft and, 126-127
  decompression chambers for, 125
  in deep-ocean mining, 161
  inflatable, 114-115
  mating hatch for, 149
  mishaps in, 120-121
  new designs for, 147-151
habitats (*cont.*)
  positioning in, 151
  for recreation, 169
  saturation diving and, 116-117
  scuba divers and, 108, 111, 126
  submersibles and, 120, 134, 149
Halley, Sir Edmund, 9-11
hard-hat divers, 31-32, 170
  salvaging by, 166
helmets, 29-32
Herodotus, 3
H. L. Hunley (submarine), 21-23
Holland, John P., 25-26
Housatonic (ship), 23

International Geophysical Year, 159

James, William H., 33
James I, king of England, 14

Kessler, Franz, 8, 9
Kumukahi (submersible), 171
Kuroshio I (submersible), 73
Kuroshio II (submersible), 74

Lake, Simon, 25, 107
Lee, Sgt. Ezra, 19-20
Lethbridge, John, 29
life-support systems:
  on research submersibles, 60-61, 66
  on work submersibles, 84-85, 90-93, 101
Lindbergh, Jon, 114
Link, Edwin A., 83, 86, 114-115, 117

Lockheed Missiles and Space Company, 90
Lulu (ship), 57

marine archaeology, 72, 167
marine biology, 75, 76, 153
Mark IV semiclosed mixed-gas scuba, 36
mining, undersea, 158-163
Mizar (submersible), 58

National Aeronautics and Space Administration, 132
natural gas, offshore drilling for, 161-163
Nautilus (nuclear submarine), 27
Nautilus (submarine), 20-21
Naval Medical Research Laboratory, 118
Navy, U.S., 98, 101, 102, 104, 132, 147, 149-150
nitrogen narcosis, 35-36, 131
nodules, 159-160
nori, 157
North American Rockwell Corporation, 79

oceanography, 144-145
  and study of food resources, 152
oil, offshore drilling for, 78, 86, 115, 161-163
open-ocean aquaculture, 155-157
Operation Tektite, 132-134

Papin, Dr. Denis, 9
Perry Submarine Builders, 83, 86
Personnel Transfer Capsule (PTC), 125, 126
Piccard, Dr. Auguste, 39-40, 42, 46, 62
Piccard, Jacques, 43-44, 62, 64-65, 69
Pisces (submersible), 89-90
plankton, 152, 155-156
Ponce de Leon, Juan, 62
Porpoise (submarine), 26
porpoises, 128-129
  use in fish farming of, 156
Problems (Aristotle), 4
Project Nekton, 43-44
propulsion systems:
  of research submersibles, 41, 50, 55-56, 59-60, 65, 70, 71
  of work submersibles, 82-83, 85-86, 88, 90-92, 101

reed snorkel, 3-4
research submersibles, 39-77
  ballast systems of, 52, 66
  communications systems of, 41-42, 45, 68
  control systems of, 56
  discoveries made by, 43-45, 53, 62, 69, 72, 167
  life-support systems of, 60-61, 66
  propulsion systems of, 41, 50, 55-56, 59-60, 65, 70, 71
  study of food sources by, 152-153
robot underwater vehicles (*see also* submersibles, unmanned), 102-106
Rosaldo (ship), 111
Rouquayrol, Benoît, 33-34

salvaging, 164-167
with diving chambers, 138-139
in work submersibles, 83, 87
saturation diving, 116-117
Scorpion (submarine), 47, 97
Scripps Institution of Oceanography, 53
scuba, 33-37
scuba divers:
commercial fishing by, 154
diving chambers for, 135-138
as fish farmers, 156
and habitats, 108, 111, 126
mishaps of, 120-121
recreational, 169
salvaging by, 165-166
and submersibles, 87
and Swimmer Sled, 95-96
Scyllis, 3-4
sea habitats, *see* habitats
Sealab projects, 116-132
sea lions, 130
self-contained underwater breathing apparatus, *see* scuba
Severyanka (submersible), 75-76
Siebe, Augustus, 30-32
snorkels:
designed by Da Vinci, 28
reed, 3-4
on submarines, 3, 14
sonar, 88-89, 90, 94, 99-100, 154
Soucoupe Sous-Marin (submersible), 48
spacecraft, 145
communication between habitats and, 126-127
Spilhaus, Dr. Athelstan, 156
Standard Underwater Research Vehicle (SURV), 76
Star I (submersible), 69-70, 120
Star II (submersible), 70
Star III (submersible), 70, 71, 79
Stenuit, Robert, 114
submarines:
ballast tanks of, 13, 17
commercial transport uses of, 163-165
development of, 12-27
losses of, 46-48, 97
nuclear, 27
snorkels on, 3, 14
tours in, 168-169
transport of submersibles by, 98, 101
undersea supply depots for, 107
underwater mining uses of, 160, 161
Submerged Object Recovery Device (SORD), 104
Submersible Portable Inflatable Dwelling (SPID), 115-116
submersibles:
experimental building materials for, 169-170
and fish farming, 156
and habitats, 120, 134
mating hatch for, 149
new designs for, 146
in new fishing methods, 153-155
recreational use of, 167-168
research, *see* research submersibles

submersibles (*cont.*)
unmanned, 102-106, 148
work, *see* work submersibles
swim fins, 28
Swimmer Sled, 94-96
Swiss National Exposition, 168-169

tektites, 134
television, closed circuit:
in habitats, 109-111, 148
for rescue missions, 99
in research submersibles, 42, 68
in work submersibles, 83, 89
Thresher (submarine), 46-48, 97, 166
torpedoes, 23, 25
first use of, 18-20
trawler submersibles, 153-154
Trieste (bathyscaphe), 39-48, 166
Trieste II (bathyscaphe), 46-48
Turtle (submarine), 16-19
Twenty Thousand Leagues Under the Sea (Verne), 24

U-boats, *see* submarines
University of Pennsylvania, 167
University of Washington, 104

Verne, Jules, 24-25

Walsh, Navy Lt. Donald, 43-44
Washington, George, 16
weather station, underwater, 124
Westinghouse Electric Corporation, 72, 135, 139, 146
wet suits, 128, 132, 136, 137
work submersibles, 79-106
ballast systems of, 82
life-support systems of, 84-85, 90-93, 101
propulsion systems of, 82-83, 88, 90-92, 101
rescue missions performed by, 87, 97-101
salvaging by, 83, 87, 165-166
unmanned, 102-106
use of television in, 83, 89
World War II:
frogmen in, 5
submarines in, 3, 25

Xerxes, 3-4

Yomiuri (submersible), 51, 74-75

ABOUT THE AUTHOR

Frank Ross, Jr., has had a successful writing career for a number of years. Among his many books for young people are studies of such varied regions as the tropic zone and Antarctica. The aerospace world has long been one of his special interests, and he has written several books on the subject. He first became interested in oceanography when he noticed some of the striking parallels between deep-sea research and the exploration of space.

The author is a native of New York City now residing on eastern Long Island. In his leisure time Frank Ross, Jr., enjoys painting, listening to music, gardening, fishing, and watching football—both collegiate and professional. He is also an avid stamp collector, quite naturally specializing in aviation and space subjects.